HOW IT ALL BEGAN
Origins of the Christian Church

O.C. Edwards, Jr.

FORWARD MOVEMENT PUBLICATIONS, CINCINNATI

When Seabury Press first published *How It All Began* in 1978 the present Book of Common Prayer was "the proposed book" and inclusive language had not yet become a major concern among authors and publishers. Forward Movement has reprinted the text of the original edition, without revision in order to keep the book's price as low as possible.

ACKNOWLEDGEMENTS

This book has its origins in a series of lectures delivered at Trinity Episcopal Church in Wauwatosa, Wisconsin. I am grateful to the Rev. George White, Rector at that time, for the invitation, and to Mrs. White for her hospitality while the lectures were being given. The task of transforming the lectures into a book was made easier by the counsel of such friends as my colleagues at Nashotah House, especially Urban T. Holmes, III, Joseph I. Hunt, and Thomas J. Talley, and W.R.K. Crockett of the Vancouver School of Theology, and Aidan Kavanaugh, O.S.B., of the University of Notre Dame.

Grateful acknowledgement is made to the following authors and publishers for permission to use copyrighted material from the sources listed:

Lutterworth, Press—H. Ringgren, *Sacrifice in the Bible*, part of the series of "World Christian Books."

Westminster Press—Cyril C. Richardson, translator and editor, *Early Christian Fathers*, vol. I of The Library of Christian Classics.

Cambridge University Press—B.S. Easton, *Apostolic Tradition.*

SPCK—Seabury Press—J. Stevenson, editor, *A New Eusebius: Documents Illustrative of the History of the Church to A.D. 337.*

Longman Group—David McKay, Inc.—J.N.D. Kelly, *Early Christian Creeds.*

Harper & Row, Publishers, Inc.—Mircea Eliade, *The Sacred and the Profane;* R.M. Grant, *The Formation of the New Testament;* Adolf Harnack, *Mission and Expansion of Christianity in the First Three Centuries.*

The Order of the Holy Cross—Bonnell Spencer, *Sacrifice of Thanksgiving.*

Illustrations on pages 85, 106, 115 and 120—all rights reserved. The Metropolitan Museum of Art.

Contents

To Jane
with compounded interest

PART I

The Quest for Origins

As a seminary professor on the brink of retirement, I find myself falling into the same mistake time and time again. When I try to illustrate a point by comparing some aspect of the 1979 edition of the Episcopal Church's Book of Common Prayer with the text in the previous edition of 1928, my students greeted me with blank stares. They do not know what I am talking about. It has been more than a decade since what I still think of as the "new" Prayer Book was adopted and for some years before that the church was involved with draft revisions. Anyone who came to seminary straight from college would not be old enough to remember using the 1928 book. Besides, less than half of all seminarians are "cradle Episcopalians." Thus what is for me the old familiar norm in the light of which everything else is to be understood is outside the experience of many students.

It is hard for anyone coming new to something to realize that what they find has not always been like that. Someone has to have been around long enough to have seen changes occur to realize that there were also changes before she or he came on the scene. With that sort of reminder, however, one can recognize that change is the law of the universe. One of the very earliest of Greek philosphers—which is to say one of the earliest of all philosphers—summed up his thought in the phrase *panta rhe*, "all things change." He argued this by saying that you cannot step into the same river twice, his point being that by the time you step in it again the current will have taken downstream the water you stepped into the first time. His disciples sharpened his point by saying that you cannot step into the same river once; the river is changing even while you are putting your foot into it. If this seemed self-evident twenty-six centuries ago, how much more so it has to be in our hectic times.

So change is the law of the universe. And this is just as true of religion as it is of anything else. While I may still think of the 1979 Prayer Book as "new," it has already had to be supplemented with additional rites that use sexually more inclusive language. In just the short time between then and now the consciousness of our culture has altered enough that such inclusivity has come to appear imperative. The extent of that change can be seen when one remembers that the same General Convention which gave the Prayer Book its preliminary approval, that of 1976, was also the one in which legislation was passed permitting the ordination of women as priests and bishops.

Other changes are going on all the time. So many of them, in fact, that any list that could be written out would probably already sound dated before it could be published in a book. At the time this is being written it appears, for instance, that the church is likely to re-think its position in relation to a number of issues relating to human sexuality. By the time this statement is read, however, all of those things may be settled—although I doubt it.

One could think of other areas of change, but we have noted enough to make our point: Change characterizes the life of the Church today. This change was undoubtedly to be expected in an age where everything else is changing too, but it is disconcerting all the same. In *Future Shock* Alvin Toffler has described the threat that so much change poses to our capacity to adapt. At a time when we are swept by a torrent of change, many have hoped that the Church would be the one island of security and stability that would help them in coping with the need to adapt elsewhere. As we have seen, such hopes are ill-placed. There is no way that we can eliminate change in the Church. Merely to rail against it accomplishes nothing. Some good may come of trying to understand it. Much has been written pro and con about all of the individual changes that are occurring now. Not so much has appeared that would set the contemporary discussion in a wider perspective, that would show, in a phrase of Richard A. Norris (*God & World in Early Christian Theology*, p. 5), that "the problem has a background and a history." Seeing how the eucharistic rite, the pattern of Christian initiation, and the role of ministers looked in the beginning can give us a lot of insight into the current discussions. What is called for, then, is an inquiry into the origins of Christian institutions, an effort to learn how it all began.

Questions about beginnings are common to all religious people and are entirely proper. They can lead to a deeper understanding of one's religion and a more meaningful practice of it. The value of such questioning was understood in the Old Testament. We see it, for example, in the story of the institution of the sacrifice of firstborn animals:

And when in time to come your son asks you, 'What does this mean?' you shall say, 'By strength of hand the Lord brought us out of Egypt, from the land of bondage. For when Pharaoh stubbornly refused to let us go, the Lord slew all the firstborn in the land of Egypt. . . . Therefore I sacrifice to the Lord all the males that first open the womb. . . .' (Exodus 13:14–15)

In the Passover seder, which Jews keep to this day, the explanation of why the commemoration is observed is given in answer to questions from the sons. The Prayer of Consecration at the eucharist includes a story of its institution by our Lord at the Last Supper. This institution narrative not only serves to justify our celebration of the eucharist today but also, in the opinion of some Christians, effects the change of bread and wine into the Body and Blood of Christ. The quest of origins, then, can be native to the religious spirit.

The quest of origins is a historical task. And that brings up the question of what history is. To the average individual the answer must seem obvious, but few people, indeed, are able to define the word. Actually, the nature of history is one of the knottiest problems of modern philosophy and theology.

In order to get some idea of the complexity of the question we need only look briefly at the ideas of two of the most important thinkers who have given attention to the question. The first of these is Leopold von Ranke (1795–1886), who has been called "the father of scientific history." As his title indicates, he worked at a time when it was believed that scientific knowledge was the highest kind of knowledge and every field of investigation strove to imitate the accuracy attained by the natural sciences. Thus von Ranke became concerned to write about the past—to use his phrase, "as it actually happened"—without any guesswork or dependence upon ancient gossip. One of the means he used to achieve this goal was to depend a great deal more on documents such as receipts, tax rolls, and the like, documents that were not based on someone's all too fallible memory, but which actually tied individuals to particular places at particular times. Thus he hoped to be able to say with assurance that a certain thing happened at a certain place at a certain time.

One of the first people to challenge von Ranke's theory successfully was R. G. Collingwood in his book, *The Idea of History*, which was published in 1946 after his death. He pointed out that the history von Ranke was interested in was a matter of names, dates, and places. This neglected, Collingwood said, the most important point of all—that history is about people. History, as he put it, is the "history of human affairs" (p. 212). He makes his point by distinguishing between the "inside" and "outside" of an event and says that the work of an historian:

may begin by discovering the outside of an event, but it can never end there; he must always remember that the event was an action, and that his main task is to think himself into this action, to discern the thought of its agent (p. 213).

In other words, we have not really begun to reconstruct the history of human beings when we have discovered only what they did and said; we must press on until we understand why they did and said these things. We must become aware of their thoughts and motives in order to come to terms with their full status as human beings.

In the long run it is not necessary for us to choose between these two theories as though they were mutually exclusive alternatives. We can agree with Collingwood that it is the inside of events that makes them worthy of human consideration. Yet we can remember that our only access to the inside of an event is through its outside. None of us is a mind-reader and we can never be sure that our idea of what a person in the past thought is what he actually thought. It is only through his actions—his words and his deeds—that we can penetrate to his thoughts. The historian, then, needs both to reconstruct what actually happened and also to interpret the human motivation of that event.

This double goal will be our aim in our efforts to discover how it all began. We will be concerned with both event and interpretation. We will ask not only when, where, how, and by whom our Christian institutions were originated, but also why. After all, our inquiry into our Christian past does not arise out of any merely antiquarian interest; we want to know the meaning of our present actions in order that we may perform them more sincerely to God's greater glory and our own deeper edification.

Before we try to see how it all began, perhaps we had better say something about the approach that will be made in trying to discover both the "inside" and "outside" of the charter events of the Church's history. Needless to say, we will base our reconstructions of the external events on the most recently acquired evidence in the hands of historians.

We will also take into consideration, as much as possible, the
interpretations made by the most capable and responsible
scholars. We will not try, however, to give a blow-by-blow
report of all the academic debates. Normally we will say
only what we think happened without going into all of the
alternative theories. But it is good for both the reader (and
the writer) to remember all the time that these alternatives
do exist. What we hope to present by way of reconstruction
will not be a final and infallible report, but only the way that
it looks from here right now. Yet even such a limited accom-
plishment is better than having made no effort at all to understand where our Christian institutions came from, and
an imperfect reconstruction is the only kind that is possible
in our present state of knowledge.

The inside of our view of Christian origins will be the
theological perspective from which it is presented. There are
tags and labels which would identify the point of view to a
specialist, but they are not important. It is the point of view
itself that matters and not what it is called. This way of looking at things arises out of a conviction that most of us think
of our religion too exclusively in terms of what it will do for
us. Consider the advantages we are told that we can get
from it! On a national level we are told that Christianity is
our best defense against Communism. On a family level we
are told that the family that prays together stays together.
On a personal level we are told that faith is the way to inward power, confident living, or peace of mind. Or, more
subtly, more spiritually, we are told that we can win salvation, go to heaven, become a saint. Whether or not these
things are true, they miss the point. The point is that religion
is about God. We become Christians to serve God, not to get
him to serve us.

What we are trying to say was put into just the right
words by a contemporary Dutch Roman Catholic theologian, a Dominican priest by the name of E. Schillebeeckx in
his book, *Christ the Sacrament of the Encounter with God:*

Religion is essentially a personal relation of man to God, of person to person; a personal encounter or a personal communing with God. It is precisely in this that the essential condition for a life truly centered on God consists. It is because God lovingly takes the initiative and comes down to meet men in grace that man lives in a condition of active and immediate communication with the one who, in this relationship, becomes the "living God" (p. 2f.).

Fr. Schillebeeckx tells us that God has taken the initiative and come down to meet us in grace. The manner in which God has done this is the most appropriate possible, the manner that is most likely to be effective. This manner is based on the fact that the most important thing about us is that we are persons. It is true that we are lumps of matter and subject to the same laws of physics that other lumps of matter are subject to. It is also true that we are blobs of protoplasm subject to the laws of biology that all other animals obey. But the most important thing about us is that we are persons and the only thing we really understand is personhood. We know what it is like to be a person because we are persons. When God took the initiative, therefore, he took it in the way that we can understand best: he came to us in the form of a human life, a life that was lived in all of the conditions of our own personhood by which we are limited. In was in the human life of Jesus of Nazareth that it became possible for interpersonal encounters between God and man to take place. He was such an encounter himself in his own person where divine and human natures were joined. He became the bridge on which God can meet with men as person to person. The sacraments we receive and in which we encounter God are made possible by the supreme sacrament, the God-man, Jesus the Christ.

But since we do not live in Palestine in the first century, it is not possible for us to have historical, personal relation with God through Jesus. Our personal encounter with God must be mediated further. It enjoys that mediation in the Church.

Perhaps we can understand that mediation best in terms of two descriptions of the Church which are used in the New Testament. In the New Testament the Church is described as both the *body* and *bride* of Christ. To call the Church the Body of Christ is to say that it serves the same function in the world today that the body of Jesus of Nazareth served two thousand years ago. (This is not to say that God the Son came down from heaven and animated the body of Jesus; that is the heresy of the Monophysites. Our Lord's human nature to which his divine nature was joined included a full and functioning human will and intellect.) In his one person of two natures, as theologians say, Jesus the Christ had all of his contacts with the men and women of his time on earth through the medium of his body. It was by means of this body that he spoke to people, healed the sick, died on the cross, and rose from the dead. He did not encounter men as a disembodied spirit. He met them and expressed his love for them through a human body. When we call the Church the Body of Christ we mean by this expression that it is the medium through which we encounter our Lord in the world today. It is in the Church that he comes to us. It is through the Church that he expresses himself for the salvation of the world. The name Body thus expresses to us the nature of the Church as the manward motion of God.

To call the Church Bride, on the other hand, is to designate her as human response to divine initiative. In this divine-human encounter man responds to God with ultimate personal adoration. Thus the distinctive and essential character of the Church is that it is interpersonal encounter between God and man. What we mean by salvation is this interpersonal relation. The Church, then, can be called a community of salvation. It is the community which has divine-human encounter as its distinctive quality of life. This, then, is the theological perspective from which our book is written. Everything in it is to be understood from this point of view. And, having stated it, we are now in position to go ahead and see how it all began.

2

The Origin of the Bible

Among the paraphernalia of the average Christian's religion, one of the items that most belongs is the Bible. The sacred Scripture of the Christians is one of the most familiar phenomena of Western culture. The Bible is the all-time bestseller among books in America. Lessons from it are read and expounded in church; much of the instruction that Christians receive in church school and elsewhere is based on it. Individual Scripture reading and study is one of the methods of private devotion most encouraged among us. Bibles are given as awards, carried by brides, quoted by orators, and placed in hotel rooms. Among certain Christian bodies the image of the book itself is regarded as a sacred symbol and often taboos are attached to the way that the Bible is handled. Small wonder, then, that the sacred book of our religion should seem so natural an element of our faith that few of us have ever thought to ask how the Bible itself came into existence and how it came to have such significance for Christians.

There are, however, good grounds for raising such questions. For one thing, Jews and Christians are among the comparatively few "religions of the book" in the world. Many faiths, especially primitive ones, have no sacred writings at all, and most of those that do have them do not hold them in such high regard as we hold ours. This is to say that the sacred writings they have do not play such a crucial role in the practice of their religion. And our own tradition existed for a number of centuries before it acquired a literature which it regarded as holy.

While the earliest event recorded in the Bible is the creation itself, the history of the Bible begins with the patriarchs Abraham, Isaac, and Jacob. This does not mean that they wrote any part of the Bible nor does it mean that they had any sacred writings. Indeed, it is utterly unlikely that they had any writing at all. But the stories we do have about them seem to come from the time when they are supposed to have lived. That time was around 2000 B.C. Archaeologists have discovered much about the sort of life men had in that region at that time and the details of daily living that we see in the patriarchal narratives coincide with those of the time these men are said to have lived. This means that the stories probably go back that far, but they were not written down at the time. Only a person who lived in a culture of plentiful books would be surprised that the stories were not preserved in writing. The way that these stories were passed down is the way that most stories in the world have been passed down— by word of mouth. It was almost a thousand years later that any writing began in Palestine that we know anything about. That was roughly the time of King David. In 2 Samuel 8:16 we read that among the officers of David's court was Jehoshaphat, the son of Ahilud, who was recorder. He is the first literate Israelite of whom we know. Perhaps it was around his time that the first efforts were made at writing down some of the stories of Israel's religious tradition.

Having stories written down about how God helped our religious ancestors does not mean, however, that we have Holy Scripture. To have a Bible we need not only a written record of holy events; we must also believe that the record itself is holy. It is possible that we know the very year in which the concept of sacred writing first entered the religion of our Hebrew forebears. The year was 621 B.C. and this is the way it happened. In the years since David, the kings had become progressively more involved in the politics of the Middle East. Among the results of this involvement was a decreased dependence upon God and an increased confidence among the kings in their ability to maneuver and negotiate and wheel and deal. In all of this diplomacy and horse trading religious concessions had been made and foreign gods had been introduced into Israel. Finally, however, a righteous king came to the throne—the *good* King Josiah, as he was called. One of the projects that he undertook was the restoration of the Temple of Jerusalem, which had fallen into disrepair. During the reconstruction a book was discovered in the Temple which contained the law of God. It was taken to the high priest who sent it to the king. The king was deeply impressed:

> Then the king sent, and all the elders of Judah and Jerusalem were gathered to him. And the king went up to the house of the Lord and with him all the men of Judah and all the inhabitants of Jerusalem and the priests and the prophets, all the people, both small and great; and he read in their hearing all the words of the book of the covenant which had been found in the house of the Lord. And the king stood by the pillar and made a covenant before the Lord . . . to perform the words of this covenant that were written in this book; and all the people joined in the covenant. (2 Kings 23:1–3)

This, then, is the first time that we have anything that can be called a Bible and it was only a small part of the Bible that we have today; most scholars think that it was some part of our present book of Deuteronomy. Nor did it serve for very long; within a quarter of a century the country was overrun and the cream of the citizenry were led away captive into the land of Babylon.

The next we hear of something like a Bible is around 440 B.C. The people had come back from captivity and rebuilt the Temple, which had been destroyed in the conquest. We are told in the eighth chapter of Nehemiah (which admittedly is one of the books of the Old Testament which raises many problems for historical reconstruction) that Ezra the priest read to the people what is called "the book of the law of Moses which the Lord had given to Israel" (8:1). It is said that the people wept when they heard the words of the law. We do not know precisely what is meant by "the book of the law of Moses" but we do know that within a short time the first five books of the Old Testament—Genesis, Exodus, Leviticus, Numbers, and Deuteronomy—were all thought to have been written by Moses and to contain God's law, his Torah. For a while, then, these five books comprised the Bible. The Samaritans broke away from the Judaism of the Temple during this period and the only Bible they have to this day is the five books of the Torah.

The next group of books to be recognized by the Jews was called the Prophets. This group includes not only Isaiah, Jeremiah, Ezekiel, and the others, but also the books we would call historical, such as Joshua, Judges, Samuel, and Kings since the Jews considered all of them prophets. The first record we have that indicates that the prophetic literature was accepted as a part of the canon of Holy Scripture comes to us from 132 B.C. A Jew had moved to Egypt as many did in this period and he taught his faith down there. As a means of instruction he wished to use a book that his grandfather had written in Hebrew. In order to make use of it he had to translate it into Greek. This book appears in our Apocrypha as Ecclesiasticus. In his prologue to the book the grandson tells us that his grandfather had devoted himself especially "to the reading of the law and the prophets and the other books of our fathers." Thus we hear the Prophets referred to in a manner that suggests that they were regarded as a part of the Bible.

You may have noticed that the writer referred not only to the Law and the Prophets but also to "the other books of our fathers." This indicates that other writings were also accepted as sacred. These are undoubtedly some of the other books of our Old Testament. We do not know, though, exactly which of them were recognized as authoritative at that time. 1 and 2 Chronicles and Ezra and Nehemiah were thought to close the period of inspiration so that nothing scriptural could be written afterwards. The Psalms were probably accepted on account of their association with the liturgy. The attribution of Proverbs to Solomon helped that book to gain recognition. A commentary on Job found with the Dead Sea Scrolls suggests that Job was regarded as canonical before 50 B.C. The book of Daniel, which is included here in the Jewish canon rather than among the Prophets because of its having been written in the time of the Maccabees, was the most rapidly canonized book of the Old Testament, undoubtedly because it was so timely. Incidentally, even though it did not appear until the time mentioned it was still thought to come from the time of the Babylonian captivity and thus before the time of Ezra and therefore was regarded as eligible to be Scripture. The other five books of the Old Testament were admitted to the canon chiefly for their association with festivals of the Jewish religious calendar: the Song of Solomon with Passover, Ruth with Pentecost, Lamentations with the Ninth of Ab (when Jerusalem fell), Ecclesiastes with Tabernacles, and Esther with Purim. The association of these books with the particular feasts took place over a long period of time.

The date that is normally given for the fixation of the Jewish canon is 90 A.D. and the occasion is referred to as the Council of Jamnia. The Jews had revolted against their Roman conquerors a little over thirty years after Jesus died. The effort was pathetic and futile and at the same time rather noble. Even the Roman historian Tacitus gave a grudging admiration for the courage of the Jews in spite of his contempt for what he could only regard as their fanatical superstition. We see it in his record of the siege of Jerusalem:

It is recorded that the beseiged, of every age and both sexes, amounted to 600,000. All who could bore arms, and the number of those who dared do so was larger than the normal proportion. Men and women showed equal perseverance: they feared life more than death if they should be forced to leave their country (*Histories* 5.11, trans. Moses Hadas).

Nevertheless, the Romans destroyed the Temple in 70 A.D. This caused the transfer of the Jewish religious center to the little town near the coast about twenty miles away called Jamnia or Jabneh. Scholars disagree over whether there was actually a meeting there or not, but it is known that the essential biblical canon of Judaism was settled on by the scholars around 90 A.D. These books are the same as those that make up the Old Testament recognized by most Protestants.

Not all Jewish religious writings were included in the list that came out of Jamnia. Some of them are what we call the Apocrypha. The Apocrypha has been called "the bridge between the Testaments." It consists of Jewish writings dating from 200 B.C. to 100 A.D. Thus they obviously come from a period later than the time of Ezra when all inspiration was thought to have ceased. We have already mentioned that there was a large colony of Jews in Egypt at that time. Many, for instance, were in the city of Alexandria at the mouth of the Nile, the second largest city in the Roman empire and its scholarly and literary capital. These Egyptian Jews did not share the Palestinian opinion that prophecy had stopped with Ezra; they thought that some of their own recent writings were also holy. The books they accepted but which the rabbis at Jamnia rejected are by and large what make up our Apocrypha. They appeared in the translation of the Old Testament into Greek which is known as the Septuagint.

If you are wondering how the Christian Scripture was begun you will no doubt be surprised to find that you already know. You know because the first Bible of Christians was the Old Testament. For our Lord and his disciples the Holy Scripture was the Hebrew Bible, but as the Church moved out

into the gentile world it became the Septuagint, the Greek
Old Testament which included the Apocrypha. By saying
that the Old Testament was the first Bible of Christians we
are saying more than just that the first Christians were Jews
who naturally revered the Jewish holy books. The earliest
Christians did not interpret the Old Testament in the same
way the Jews did; it did not mean the same thing to them.
The Christians believed that the Old Testament prophesied
Christ. In almost any place you read in the New Testament
there are quotations from the Old in abundance and they are
all seen as foretelling Christ. The first Christian missionaries
invoked numerous passages from the Jewish Scripture to
prove that Jesus was the Messiah whom the Jews had been
expecting. This general method of biblical interpretation,
which understood ancient narratives to be predictions of later events, was not unusual among the Jews; the community
that produced the Dead Sea Scrolls, for instance, used it
extensively. The difference in Christian interpretation was
not so much in method as in finding in Jesus the key that
opened the meaning of the Old Testament.

As we said, gentile Christians used the Greek Old Testament. Since this fact is important we had better go into it a
little more. We can begin with the name Septuagint, the
Latin word for *seventy*. The name comes from a legend
which is told in an ancient document known as the *Letter
of Aristeas* and in other places. The legend has·it that King
Ptolemy Philadelphus (285–247 B.C.) was building up the
magnificent library at Alexandria and he was advised to procure for it a copy of the sacred books of the Jews. The king,
therefore, wrote the high priest in Jerusalem and, after in-
gratiating himself by referring to favors he had done the
Jews, requested the high priest to send him capable Jewish
scholars who could translate the Torah into Greek. The story
has it that the high priest chose six scholars from each of the
twelve tribes, which made a total of seventy-two. The number was rounded off to seventy and thus the translators are

referred to as the Seventy and their translation is called the Septuagint. The story goes on to say that the task was completed in seventy-two days. A later variant makes it even more miraculous and says that the men were divided into thirty-six pairs, each to produce an independent translation, and they all came up with identical results.

It is unfortunate that so nice a story cannot be believed. The likelihood is that the translation was produced by the Jewish community in Alexandria, which was beginning to need a translation to read its own Bible because it no longer understood Hebrew. It is also probable that the original translation was of only the first five books of the Old Testament, the Torah, and that the rendering of the other books took as long as 150 years to complete and may not have been finished by the time of Jesus. This long process of creating a Bible in Greek meant that the list of books that made it up was indefinite for an extended period of time. Since the Jews in Alexandria and, later on, the Christians too recognized as inspired some of the books that had been written there and elsewhere in Greek or had been translated into Greek, the number of books in the canon of the Septuagint is greater than that in the list of Jamnia. Most of the extra books in the Greek canon are included in the Old Testament in Roman Catholic editions of the Bible, are printed between the Testaments as the Apocrypha in Anglican and Lutheran editions, and are left out of most others. It must be noted that the Hebrew canon was not decided upon until near the close of the first Christian century; one of their purposes in excluding apocryphal books was that Christians found them useful in supporting their defenses against the Jews.

THE NEW TESTAMENT

The earliest Christian writings we know of are the letters St. Paul wrote to the churches that he founded. But we may be sure that St. Paul had no idea that he was writing biblical books when he wrote those letters. He had a far humbler evaluation of them. He would be at work getting a church started in one city and word would come to him that a church he had already founded was having difficulties of one sort or another. He was too committed where he was to be able to drop everything and hurry over. The best that he could do under the circumstances was to write a letter, and the letters that he wrote to local churches to relay his advice in particular crises have been guiding the Church ever since as the Epistles of St. Paul.

We do not really know how the letters first came to be collected. A number of theories have been advanced but none of them has been able to command universal assent. One of the most interesting theories, associated with E. J. Goodspeed, calls attention to the fact that we do not find Christian writers quoting St. Paul until after the time when the Acts of the Apostles must have been published. Since about half of the Book of Acts is about St. Paul, it may be that its appearance interested someone enough in St. Paul to make that person want to collect his letters. We even have a guess as to the possible identity of that person. One of St. Paul's letters was written to ask a master to be kind to a runaway slave whom Paul had persuaded to return. The master was Philemon and the name of the slave was Onesimus. About fifty years later we hear of someone named Onesimus who was at that time bishop of Ephesus. The conjecture is that the slave became a bishop and collected the letters out of gratitude to the apostle who had befriended him. There are several objections that have been offered to this theory, among them that the Book of Acts does not mention St. Paul's letters and that the theory presupposes both less communication between the churches at that time and less appreciation of the letters of St. Paul than there must actually have been. At any rate we know that the letters were collected during this period and began to appear together in a

single manuscript. We also know that these letters were regarded as a part of the Bible before the last book in the New
Testament was written. That book was 2 Peter and it was
probably written 120–150 A.D. by a Christian who thought
he was saying what Peter would have said to the Church of
his generation. In 2 Peter 3:16–17 we read:

So also our beloved brother Paul wrote to you according to the
wisdom given to him, speaking of this as he does in all of his
letters. There are some things in them hard to understand, which
the ignorant and unstable twist to their destruction as they do the
other Scriptures.

Even before St. Paul wrote there were already Christian
words that were thought to possess the highest authority.
These, of course, were the words of Jesus. We get a hint of
this in Acts 20:35 where St. Paul is quoted as "remembering
the words of the Lord Jesus." We also find allusions to the
sayings of Jesus in James and 1 Peter. There is abundant evidence that these sayings were circulated by word of mouth
for quite a long time after they had been written down in
the Gospels. Our point, here, however, is that these words
of our Lord were regarded as authoritative in the Church
well before they were written down and before it had occurred to Christians that any writings they had produced
could have authority as great as that of the Old Testament.

Scholars who have made comparative studies of the Gospels have come to a number of interesting conclusions. For
example, they are rather certain that the first Gospel to be
written was Mark; they place the date around 68 A.D. And
they have become convinced that Matthew and Luke had
copies of Mark open before them when they wrote their
Gospels, and that they drew much of their material from his
work. These scholars have also noticed that Matthew and
Luke have another source in common, a collection of the sayings of Jesus (which for convenience they designate "Q" for
the German word *Quelle*, meaning *source*). In addition to

these two common sources, Matthew and Luke each have their own private sources of information. The significance of this for us is that the sayings of Jesus were collected before the Gospels were written. For a number of reasons we think they were collected before 50 A.D., which is less than twenty years after the Resurrection.

Not everything the evangelists incorporated into their gospels came to them from earlier sources, however. Some of their material they wrote themselves as a way of bringing out their own understanding of the significance of Jesus. Mark, for instance, was the man who invented the literary form of the gospel. There was nothing like it in earlier Jewish or Greco-Roman biographical literature, since its purpose was neither to satisfy curiosity nor to edify, but to show how God had acted decisively in Jesus for the reclamation of a lost world. A gospel, then, was written to convert its reader to belief in Jesus. Mark's difficulty in fitting together all of the single stories that had been passed down by word of mouth and of subordinating them to the major story of Jesus' death and resurrection was that each separate story was already the whole gospel in a nutshell. Each miracle recounted and every authoritative pronouncement passed down already implied the unique status of Jesus, and Mark had to see that none of them "gave away the plot" before the climax of the Passion narrative was reached. He did this by showing that no one had really understood any of the earlier demonstrations of who Jesus was, so the revelation remained to be made in the events of Holy Week.

There were also special problems confronting Matthew and Luke in the writing of their gospels. Matthew appears to have been fighting on two fronts: he had to deal with Jews who said that his Jewish-Christian congregation had abandoned the law of Moses and he had to answer gentiles who said that Christians were not bound by any of the Hebrew laws. He responded to the first by saying that Jesus had not come to destroy the law, but to fulfill it (5:17). It was fulfilled by interpreting it always in the light of the law of love as that is expressed in the golden rule (7:12) and the summary of the law (22:37–40). His insistence that the law was still in effect, even if the principle for interpreting it had changed, was also answer to those who said that it no longer applied.

Luke was dealing with a different problem and he edited his gospel to emphasize his solution to it. Before his time most Christians had expected the immediate return of Jesus, and when Luke began to write fifty or sixty years after the Ascension, the faith of many Christians was growing cold because of the delay in the second coming. Luke wrote his gospel to prove that God had never intended for·the world to end so soon; he had intended for time to go on long enough for the Church to spread throughout the world. In order to make this point Luke continued his gospel into a second volume that told of the expansion of the Church into the non-Jewish world as far as Rome, under the impetus of the Holy Spirit. This second volume is the Acts of the Apostles, and it is the first history of the Church we have.

So far we have discussed only three gospels and yet everyone knows there are four. The reason we have postponed mentioning the Gospel according to St. John is that it is different from the other three. One way of approaching that difference is to call the first three gospels the "synoptic gospels." Synoptic comes from the Greek and means "capable of being seen together." This means that the first three gospels may be set down in parallel columns and compared. This is because both Matthew and Luke used much of Mark and also shared the Q source, as we saw above. John drew on a different strand of tradition about Jesus and he also used his material differently. Instead of merely quoting short, incisive statements from Jesus, he expanded them into long and ordered speeches. He also correlated them with the stories he told so that the symbolic meaning of an event was developed in the discourse that followed. This, together with his use of a special theological vocabulary that contrasted light and darkness, truth and falsehood, life and death as the alternatives between which men must choose, was the reason that Clement of Alexandria suggested at the beginning of the third century that "John, as the last, because he perceived that the corporeal things are presented in the (synoptic) gospels, at the exhortation of his friends and impelled by the divine Spirit, wrote a spiritual gospel" (quoted in Eusebius, *History of the Christian Church* 6.14.17).

The writing of the Gospels was originally done not with the intention of writing books of the Bible, but with a desire to preserve the traditions about Jesus' words and deeds. Probably all four Gospels were completed before the end of the first century, but that does not mean that they were circulated through out the Church yet or that they were considered to be Holy Scripture. At first a Gospel may have been thought to be inspired only in the area in which it was written—Rome, Ephesus, Antioch, or Caesarea—but gradually all the Gospels became known and accepted everywhere. Maybe this process had already begun before the New Testament was completed. In 1 Timothy 5:18 we read: "The Scripture says . . . the laborer deserves his wages." This is a quotation of Luke 10:7. In another early Christian work, one of the earliest we have outside the New Testament, since it was probably written between 100 and 150 A.D., we have a quotation from either Mark or Matthew that is introduced by the formula: "another scripture also says" (2 Clement 2:4). Thus some, at least, of the Gospels must have been regarded as Scripture by then. There were early heretics, however, who did not like the idea of four Gospels, so some of them tried to get rid of all but one and others tried to blend the four together into one. By about 183 A.D., though, Irenaeus, one of the greatest of early Christian writers, can speak as though four were the naturally inevitable number of Gospels:

Since there are four zones of the world in which we live and four principal winds . . . it is fitting that (the Church) should have four pillars, breathing out immortality on every side and vivifying men afresh (*Refutation of All Heresies* III. xi. 8, Ante-Nicene Fathers translation).

By this time, then, the basic shape of the canon of the New Testament was generally agreed upon. Or, as R. P. C. Hanson has put it, "We might describe the canon as a circle of light with dazzling light at the center and twilight at the edges" (*Tradition in the Early Church*, p. 246). Bit by bit the Church agreed upon which of the other early Christian writings should and which should not be included in their Bible.

When discussing the Old Testament we saw that books written after the time of Ezra could be considered canonical only if they were thought to have been written *before* the time of Ezra. A similar principle was applied by the early Church to the New Testament. Books were recognized to be canonical that were believed to have been written by either an Apostle or the companion of an Apostle. Modern scholars know that in almost no case except the major Pauline epistles was this assignment of authorship correct, but it still was the basis for admission to the canon. Since we now know that many of the books that were supposed to have been written by Apostles actually weren't, our modern reaction is to regard them as forgeries and assume that such deception is inconsistent with sincere religion. In responding this way we are imposing modern standards on an ancient people who did not look at things the same way. The Jews had a strong sense of what has been called "corporate personality"; they felt that members of a group shared the same spirit and that any member of a group around a great leader could legitimately speak in his name. Those who wished to give his message to later generations wrote in the leader's name, so that the spirit of his message would be regarded as genuine.

We do not have to share this attitude, but we do have to understand it in the ancients if we are ever to comprehend the process of canonizing the Bible.

One of the clearest cases of the theory of corporate personality in the New Testament canon is in the Johannine literature. It is obvious that the fourth Gospel, the three epistles of John, and the Revelation all represent the same school of thought, but most investigators do not think that all of these documents were written by the same man. Most would say that the purest expression of the thought of the founder of the Johannine "school" is in the Gospel according to St. John (although there is considerable disagreement about the relation of that founder to the Apostle John, the son of Zebedee). Yet even this gospel gives evidence of some editorial re-working by a member of the school, as for example, in John 21:24: "He is the disciple who spoke of these things, the one who also wrote them down; and we know that what he said is true." This line was obviously written by someone other than the author of the rest of the book. It is possible that the follower of the founder who revised the gospel was also the author of the three Johannine letters, since their thought is remarkably close to that of the founder, but there are minute differences of style. The letters come from an "elder" (*presbyteros*) who oversees several congregations that are troubled by heretics denying that Jesus had a real human body (1 John 4:2–3).

There are many similarities of thought—and as many differences—between these Johannine works and the Revelation that is attributed to St. John the Divine. This mysterious book, claiming to derive from a vision on the island of Patmos, is in the same apocalytic or revelatory style as the book of Daniel in the Old Testament. Addressed to seven churches near the Aegean coast of what is modern Turkey (an area of great cultural achievement at the time), the Revelation is stated in the form of a heavenly vision but is probably best understood as a warning to Christians that they will suffer persecution in the near future for their refusal to participate in the Roman emperor-worship making headway in that area at the time. This book probably came from a circle that had close ties with whoever wrote the fourth Gospel and the Johannine epistles.

More directly pseudonymous were the Pastoral epistles—1 & 2 Timothy and Titus—since they have no real appearance of having been written by St. Paul or by anyone who was closely associated with him. Yet they do claim to be letters written by him to two of his assistants whom he left in charge of work in Ephesus and Crete. The main problems dealt with in these letters are false teachers and the organization of the Christian community; we are told about the offices of bishop, elder, and deacon, but we are told more about the moral qualities of those who hold these jobs than we are told about their duties. Quite apart from the theological and stylistic differences between these works and the genuine letters of St. Paul, there is also a difference in tone. The kinds of problems faced are not those dealt with by Paul in his lifetime, but are much more those of a generation later. For that reason the Pastorals are usually assigned to an anonymous admirer of St. Paul who lived in the last decade of the first Christian century.

Even less Pauline is the Epistle to the Hebrews. The whole method of doing theology is entirely different. This work appears to be strongly influenced by the Judaism of Alexandria in Egypt, which was a very Hellenized kind of Judaism. Jewish theologians in Alexandria had learned the allegorical method from the Greek interpreters of Homer there and had appropriated this method for the interpretation of the Old Testament. The author of Hebrews is writing to a congregation of Jewish Christians who were in danger of lapsing back into Alexandrian Judaism, and he points out to them the danger of doing so by using the theological methods they are so enamored with. Ironically enough, it was the early Christian theologians of Alexandria, using the literary-critical techniques of that city, who pointed out that the style of this work is different from that of St. Paul. Most Eastern Christians liked the Platonizing tone of Hebrews and were anxious to regard it as Pauline so that it could be included in the canon. Western church leaders, though, were hesitant because Hebrews takes a hard line with lapsed Christians, and they were afraid that it would furnish ammunition to divisive elements in the West who wanted to be harsh with Christians whose faith had wavered under persecution. Thus it did not gain acceptance there until the fourth century.

The general or catholic (in the sense of being for everyone) epistles—James, 1 & 2 Peter, and Jude—claim to be written by two of our Lord's relatives and by the chief of the Apostles, claims that are disputed by the majority of New Testament scholars. James shows many signs of having been written by someone with an excellent Greek literary education, a commodity that seems unlikely to have been available in Nazareth. It is a disjointed collection of material in the form of the popular sermons of Cynic and Stoic preachers and it mentions the name of Jesus only twice, but its Christian character is very clear from the frequent allusions to sayings of Jesus. In part it seems directed against a perverted Paulinism that misunderstood the doctrine of justification by faith preached by the Apostle to the gentiles. 1 Peter is also in excellent Greek that hardly seems in character for a Galilean fisherman; it appears to be a sermon for a baptismal service that has been recycled into a letter to Christians in danger of persecution. 2 Peter appears to be the last book in the New Testament to be written, dating from 120–50 A.D., and is a defense of the earlier Christian expectation of the immediate second coming of Jesus. It is based on the epistle of Jude, which was more concerned with false teaching. All four of these were quite slow to gain wide recognition in the canon.

We can say this with certainty because we have a list, called the Muratorian fragment, which comes to us from the end of the second century and is written in very bad Latin. It names twenty-two of the twenty-seven books we now recognize as scriptural, and the five left out—James, 1 and 2 Peter, 3 John, and Hebrews—are not among those we consider most important. A later theologian divided books into three categories: accepted, rejected, and doubtful. The doubtful are those that are recognized in some churches but not in others and the two categories of accepted and doubtful include all the books in our New Testament. The earliest list we have that matches ours exactly was by St. Athanasius and comes from his thirty-ninth festal letter of the year 367. Shortly afterwards the African councils of Hippo (393) and Carthage (397) gave synodical approval to the same list and most Christians ever since have accepted these twenty-seven as their own sacred books. They go with the Jewish Scripture to make up our Bible.

The history of the canon as we have related it has been largely "outside history." We have said much about how the books came to be recognized as scriptural but very little about the content which was the basis of their selection. The first thing to be said about this content is that the subject of the Bible is the action of God in history—from Abraham, Isaac, and Jacob to Peter and Paul, but most especially in Jesus Christ. The God Christians worship is not one whose existence they have arrived at as the end of a long process of reason, but the one whom they and their religious ancestors have encountered in their own lives, directing their personal histories and the history of the world to the triumphant goal of his gracious will. The second point is that the story of how we got our Bible shows that God also gave it to us through historical process. Our Bible is not thought to be like the *Book of Moroni* which Mormons believe was copied from golden plates that Joseph Smith found in the ground after their location was revealed to him. It was rather written by men who did not know they were writing scripture and what they wrote may not have been recognized to contain divine revelation until centuries later. The third point is a conclusion drawn from the first two: since we have seen that God reveals himself in history—both in the history contained in the Bible and the history of how we got the Bible—we may expect him to be active in history today: world history, church history, our parochial history, and our personal history. In other words, the history of the Bible, as it was written, canonized, and is read in the Church today, is a history of encounter between God and men. R. M. Grant summed it up this way:

It may seem that we are treating the New Testament and the Church as human products and nothing more. Admittedly and certainly, we are treating them as human products, for this is what they indisputably are. But from the standpoint of Christian theology there are no products of this kind that are not human. The 'divine initiative' can doubtless exist apart from human responses (the creation of the universe provides an obvious example), but the life of the Church and the witness of the new Testament books cannot (theologically speaking) be viewed as in any sense divine apart from their 'humanity'. The 'divine-human encounter' has to be a real encounter with two parties involved (*The Formation of the New Testament*, pp. 185f.).

3

The Creeds of Christians

For at least half of the Christian centuries it would have seemed absurd to ask how we got our creeds because it would have been assumed that we knew very well how we got at least the Apostles Creed: it was given to us by the apostles. Here is the story as it is told in a Christian document dating from the eighth century:

On the tenth day after the Ascension when the disciples were gathered together for fear of the Jews, the Lord sent the promised Paraclete upon them. At his coming they were inflamed like red-hot iron and, being filled with the knowledge of all languages, they composed the creed. Peter said, I believe in God the Father almighty . . . maker of heaven and earth . . . Andrew said, and in Jesus Christ His Son . . . our only Lord . . . James said, Who was conceived by the Holy Spirit . . . born from the Virgin Mary . . . John said, suffered under Pontius Pilate . . . was crucified, dead, and buried . . . Thomas said, descended into hell . . . on the third day he rose again from the dead . . . James said, ascended to heaven . . . sits on the right hand of God the Father almighty . . . Philip said, thence he will come to judge the living and the dead . . . Bartholomew said, I believe in the Holy Spirit . . . Matthew said, the holy catholic Church . . . the communion of saints . . . Simon said, the remission of sins . . . Thaddeus said, the resurrection of the flesh . . . Matthias said, eternal life (quoted by J. N. D. Kelly, *Early Christian Creeds,* p. 3).

Everyone in the West believed this legend until the time of the Council of Florence in the middle of the fifteenth century, when the Greek and Latin speaking churches were making their last major effort to get back together. The Eastern bishops said they had never heard of this creed before—if it had really been given by the apostles it would be mentioned in the Book of Acts in the New Testament, and Christians everywhere would have it, not just those in the West. By the time of the Reformation almost everyone had stopped believing that the apostles had written a creed, though the idea was slow dying out in some circles. That left the Church with the question we now face: how did we get our creeds?

No creed as such is written out in the New Testament. That does not mean, however, that the first Christians had no distinctive beliefs. If they had lacked any, the Church would never have existed. The most distinctive Christian doctrine was that Jesus was the Messiah long awaited by the Jews. It is expressed by simple statements—one clause confessions that Jesus is the Messiah or, to use the Greek form of the same word, Jesus is the Christ. This confession of faith was sometimes varied to include the assumption that the Messiah was divine. Jesus was called Lord, one of the Old Testament titles for God the Father. When the Church began to move out into the gentile world, these Jewish expressions had little meaning for the new audience of the Christian messages, and so terms that expressed the nearest Greek equivalents to the same ideas were used. Needless to say, the early Christian preaching about Jesus said more than this; it generally included a brief outline of his saving work. It said at least that he was crucified, that he rose from the dead, and ascended into heaven. It will have been noticed that the second paragraph of the creed today is basically such a summary of the life, death, and resurrection of Jesus. And, of course, Christian preaching was not about Jesus exclusively. It also included the proclamation of the God of the Old Testament, the God whom Jesus called Father. There were, in addition, affirmations about the Holy Spirit of God.

The reason we know that early Christian preaching included all of this is that all of it appears in the New Testament. In many, many places we have short little credal scraps such as "Jesus is the Lord" or "Jesus is the Christ." C. H. Dodd, one of the greatest of recent British New Testament scholars, has suggested that not only the sermons recorded in the New Testament, but even the basic pattern of the Gospels follows a thumbnail sketch of the life of Jesus such as we find in the second articles of the creed. A case in point is a sermon St. Peter is said to have preached in Caesarea:

You know the word which (God) sent to Israel, preaching the good news of peace by Jesus Christ (he is Lord of all), the word which was proclaimed throughout all Judea, beginning from Galilee after the baptism which John preached: how God annointed Jesus of Nazareth with the Holy Spirit and with power; how he went about doing good and healing all that were oppressed by the devil, for God was with him. And we are witnesses to all that he did both in the country of the Jews and in Jerusalem. They put him to death by hanging him on a tree; but God raised him on the third day and made him manifest . . . (Acts, 10:36–40).

There is more but we have seen enough to discern the credal shape. It is a pattern that recurs again and again in the New Testament. And these credal scraps are not just about Jesus; sometimes they include God the Father and at times the Holy Spirit also. One of these trinitarian formulas occurs at the end of the Gospel according to St. Matthew: "Go therefore and make disciples of all nations, baptizing them in the name of the Father and of the Son and of the Holy Spirit" (28:19). Another is in St. Paul's closing remarks in his second letter to the church at Corinth: "The grace of our Lord Jesus Christ, and the love of God and the fellowship of the Holy Spirit be with you all" (13:14). This is the familiar grace at the end of Daily Morning and Eve-

ning Prayer. Thus we see that while we have no creeds as
such in the New Testament, we do have the raw materials
from which creeds are made.

We can think of a number of situations in the early Church
in which it would have been useful to have the sort of suc-
cinct summary of the main tenets of Christian belief that we
have in the creeds. It would have been useful in preaching,
in worship, and in the training of candidates for admission
into the Church. It would also have come in handy in the defense of the faith against pagans and heretical Christians.
Among the many possible uses, the creeds are associated
most closely with baptism. Initiation into the Body of Christ
was regarded as the occasion *par excellence* for the confession of faith in Christ. It appears, though, that the earliest
baptismal creed was not one continuous affirmation of
faith as our creeds are today. Rather it was a series of questions and answers. We have a rather full description of how
baptism was administered in Rome in about 200 A.D. At
first, selections from the Bible were read and explained.
After the water was blessed the candidates removed their
clothes and then renounced the devil and all his works. Next
they stepped down into the font (usually having a depth of
eighteen inches of water) and the bishop or priest officiating
put his hand on the head of the candidate and asked, "Dost
thou believe in God the Father Almighty?" When the candidate replied, "I believe," water was poured over him once.
Then he was asked:

Dost thou believe in Christ Jesus, the Son of God, who was born
of the Holy Ghost of the Virgin Mary, and was crucified under
Pontius Pilate, and was dead and buried, and rose again on the
third day, alive from the dead, and ascended into heaven, and
sat at the right hand of the Father, and will come to judge the
quick and the dead?

When he replied that he did believe, water was poured on
him again. Then he was asked: "Dost thou believe in the

Holy Ghost, and the Holy Church and the resurrection of
the flesh?" After he assented, water was poured on him a
third time.

How then did we move from this interrogatory form of
the creed to what might be called a declaratory form of the
creed? The answer seems to arise from the conviction in
those days that baptism was nothing to be entered into
lightly. In the fourth century preparation for it lasted all
through Lent. During the first five weeks the candidates were
instructed in how to interpret the Bible both literally and
spiritually. The subject of instruction for the next two weeks
was the creed. During Easter week after the initiation had
already taken place the sacraments were explained. Lent
then lasted for eight weeks. After the creed had been
learned in the sixth and seventh weeks, each candidate had
to repeat it to the bishop on the Saturday before Palm Sunday to show that he had learned it by heart. Holy Week itself was so taken up with services that there was no time for
instruction then. The way this procedure seems to have
evolved is this: first the old interrogatory form was taken as
the outline for the preparation of candidates for baptism.
Then, for teaching purposes, the affirmative or declaratory
form of the creed was developed as a summary of the instruction. Thus it was taught to the candidates before it was
explained and then they had to recite it at their baptism. At
first these creeds were probably drawn up locally, and recitation of them was probably almost extemporaneous. The
creed in a given place tended to settle into a fixed pattern.
Rural and suburban churches probably adopted the creeds
of nearby metropolitan churches. By commenting on these
credal differences we do not mean to suggest that there were
essential differences of belief between the churches. The
only variations we point to are in the phraseology by which
the common faith was expressed. What we call the Apostles
Creed is a development of the old baptismal creed used at
Rome.

How did we move from having a more or less local creed to a creed that was accepted as authoritative throughout the whole Church? To answer this question we must move on to consider another function of creeds, that of serving as tests of orthodoxy. Creeds did not have this use from their very beginning; they acquired this function in the days when the Roman Empire began to grow weak. The emperors tried to bolster the sagging strength of the empire by unifying the people around their old religion, which was not followed very closely any more. Christians, of course, could not cooperate in this; that is one reason that the Church was persecuted. Even persecution, however, could not stamp out Christianity. It almost seemed to have the opposite effect. In fact, one early Christian called the blood of Christians *seed*: "the oftener we are mown down by you, the more in number we grow" (Tertullian, *Apology* 50, Ante-Nicene Fathers translation).

Early in the fourth century Constantine decided that if the empire could not be united without the Christians, he would unite it around them. He became a Christian himself. This does not mean that his conversion was entirely political and insincere. He probably was very honest in his belief, but that belief, with equal probability, was not very profound. He may have accepted Christianity because that religion had proved itself over the old Roman religion by its superior staying power. The real God must be behind a religion like that, and that was the kind of God that Constantine wanted on his side.

Constantine became a Christian in order to unite the empire around the faith, but he soon discovered that Christianity itself was not united. Most of the trouble was coming out of Egypt. The only way Constantine knew to unite the Church so that it could help him unite the empire was to call all the bishops together and let them see if they could settle their differences. When they came to an agreement they could express that agreement in the form of a creed.

In the long run the plan worked, but the long run ran
longer than Constantine had hoped; it took, in fact, 126
years. The troubles began, as we said, in Egypt—with a
priest there named Arius. Arius believed in theological "literalism"—that is, he thought, for instance, that if God the
Father is Father of God the Son, God the Son must be
younger than God the Father. This is the kind of literalism
described by C. S. Lewis when he said that some people
think that because our Lord said that we should be like
doves, we ought to lay eggs (*Mere Christianity*, p. 106).
Anyway, Arius thought that God the Father existed before
God the Son, that there was a time when God the Son did not
exist. Arius went so far as to incorporate this idea into one
of the first singing commercials. He taught his followers to
sing a little ditty in Greek that went something like this:
En hote hoti ouk en—"There was a time that he did not
exist." There was another theologian in Alexandria, Athanasius, who saw what this would do to the faith. It would mean
that the Son was not eternal as the Father was. Thus he
would be subordinate to the Father and inferior to him. He
would be less than God. And if he were less than God he
would be incapable of saving us from sin and death. In this
way Athanasius proved that Arianism would destroy Christianity. He was able to demonstrate this to the satisfaction
of the bishops at the council. Then they proceeded to draw
up a creed that would exclude Arian belief. They took a local
baptismal creed and added clauses to it that no Arian could
sign his name to. The clauses said that Jesus the Christ was
"true God of true God" or "very God of very God" as the
archaic English of the Book of Common Prayer has it. They
say that he is "begotten, not made." This means that he is not
a creature, but is of the same category of being as the Father,
in no way subordinate or inferior. The real clincher, however, is the Greek word *homoousios,* which we translate
"being of one substance with the Father." This is to say that
the Father and the Son are not only equally God, they are

both the same God. This no Arian could ever say and so the creed of this council was successful as a test of orthodoxy. That council was held at a place near Constantinople called Nicaea and for that reason the creed is called Nicene.

Yet the creed we say today at the Eucharist and call Nicene is not the creed written at that first ecumenical council in 325. That creed is the one that appeared in the council of Constantinople in 381 and was reaffirmed and strengthened at the council of Chalcedon in 451. It was rightly believed to state the faith of Nicaea a little plainer than even the creed from Nicaea stated it. It is now the only creed that is shared by Eastern and Western Christendom, with but one variation. There is another ancient creed which has a part in the English liturgy but which was never incorporated into the American Prayer Book. This creed is called the Athanasian Creed, under the mistaken notion that it was written by St. Athanasius, or the *Quincunque vult* from the first two words that appear in its Latin version. It originated in Gaul around 500 A.D. Objections to it have been raised on the basis of its damnatory clauses but even these have been defended to a certain degree by J. N. D. Kelly, one of the greatest students of the creeds and the one on whose work this chapter is largely based. He says:

In spite of the off-putting terms in which they are expressed, the true significance of the damnatory clauses lies in the reminder they give of the awful responsibility of making the right decision in matters of fundamental belief (*The Athanasian Creed*, p. 126).

This pretty well covers how we got our creeds in the first place, but one observation needs to be made about their present-day use. We have noted that the Nicene Creed is the universal eucharistic creed, which is to say that in at least the liturgies of the Eastern Orthodox, Roman Catholic, and Anglican Communions it is the creed recited at the Eucharist. The Apostles Creed is said at daily offices such as Anglican Morning and Evening Prayer. The rubric in the English

Prayer Book directs the recitation of the *Quicunque vult* at Morning Prayer on Christmas, Epiphany, Easter, Ascension, Whitsunday, and Trinity Sunday and upon certain saints' days. This means that the creeds are acts of worship. As we have them they were originally designed to be an outline for the ancient equivalent of "confirmation classes" and a test of orthodoxy to exclude people who had difficulty in accepting their dogmatic statements. Although the faith of the creeds is true, the use of the creeds in our worship is not basically pedagogical or exclusivistic. Their recitation is rather, as we said, an act of worship. They list the things for which we give thanks and praise to God. As Massey Shepherd says:

They are positive affirmations of the truth revealed to us in the Holy Scriptures. They are reminders of the promises of faith in God and in His Christ and Holy Spirit that we made in our Baptism, when we were made members of Christ in His holy Church (*The Worship of the Church*, pp. 38f.).

Thus the creeds state the ground for our hope and become a hymn of our praise and thanksgiving. Their message is expressed in the liturgy for Trinity Sunday: "Father, Son, and Holy Ghost, one God; O come let us adore him."

4

Houses of Worship

There is an idea prevalent—formed largely from spectacular religious movies made with casts of thousands, living color, and underclad actresses—that early Christians, in constant fear of their lives because of persecution, lived in underground caverns called catacombs. While it is true that Christianity was an illegal religion for the first three centuries of its existence, this does not mean that the laws against it were universally, constantly, and consistently enforced. Official persecution of Christians under orders of the emperors was a rather rare thing and whenever there was danger to the Church it came more often from local opposition roused to mob violence. There was, thus, always the possibility that faith would have to be sealed with martyrdom, but the number of Christians from whom this last full measure of devotion was actually exacted was relatively small. Anomalies were common: St. Ignatius, for instance, on his way from his church in Syria to martyrdom in Rome some time around 115 A.D. was allowed to stop and visit with churches along the way and carry on a correspondence with them without, apparently, bringing any of their members into jeopardy. Most of the time Christians could live out their lives and practice their religion in relative tranquility, although undoubtedly they did not advertise their doing so too openly.

What, then, about the catacombs? There were such things and they came into existence in this way: about the beginning of the Christian era Romans stopped cremating their dead and began to bury them. Cemeteries, however, took up a great deal of space and so in the second century the practice began around Rome and Naples of excavating underground galleries for burial in *tufa*, a soft volcanic rock there. These underground burial places were the catacombs and it was largely through Christian initiative that they were developed. Following a pagan custom, Christians would have memorial meals at the graves of their beloved dead. These meals were neither the daily bread of people living in the catacombs nor were they the Eucharist. It is possible, however, that during a rare period of intense persecution Christians would resort to the catacombs for their Eucharist where the Roman respect for the dead would protect them to a degree. We cannot stress too strongly, though, that regular Christian worship in a catacomb was an unusual rather than an ordinary occurrence.

Religious people—Christians and others—erect buildings as part of their piety. This is based on the principle of "sacred space," so called by Mircea Eliade, who has what amounts to a genius for interpreting religious phenomena. He says: "For religious man, space is not homogeneous; he experiences interruptions, breaks in it; some parts of space are qualitatively different from others" (*The Sacred and the Profane*, p. 20). These "different" spaces are the sacred ones, the ones in which a god manifests himself or in which the holy is encountered in regular worship. The rationale implicit to this principle is that sacred spaces are places where men draw near to the gods. In other words, men have access to ultimate reality in sacred spaces and they go to these spaces out of a desire to escape all that is unreal about this world and to re-found their lives in that which is completely real. Thus the significance of the church building was expressed by Eliade in this way:

For a believer, the church shares in a different space from the street in which it stands. The door that opens on the interior of the church actually signifies a solution of continuity. The threshold that separates the two spaces also indicates the distance between two modes of being, the profane and the religious. The threshold is the limit, the boundary, the frontier that distinguishes and opposes two worlds—and at the same time the paradoxical place where these two worlds communicate, where passage from the profane to the sacred world becomes possible (*The Sacred and the Profane*, p. 25).

All this is to say that there is more to religious buildings than the idea that worship has to be held somewhere and so it would be more convenient to own a place where one can worship; the building itself is felt to participate in the sphere of the sacred which is encountered in it. The general sense of the sacredness of a certain space is by no means strange to the Judeo-Christian tradition. A classic statement of the concept is Jacob's remark upon waking from his dream of a ladder that stretched from earth to heaven: "Surely the Lord is in this place! This is none other than the house of God, and this is the gate of heaven" (Genesis 28:16–17). Moses at the burning bush seemed to hear God say to him, "Do not come near; put off your shoes from your feet, for the place on which you are standing is holy ground" (Exodus 3:5).

One would expect that early Christian buildings might have been modeled on the edifices of other faiths that were in use during the period when our religion got its start. Investigation, however, does not bear out that expectation entirely. The majority of sacred buildings up to that time had been temples and, unlike churches, temples are not places in which congregations gather for services of worship. A temple is essentially a shrine constructed to house a cult object—usually an image of the deity in honor of whom the temple is constructed. (The Temple at Jerusalem was to some degree an exception to this rule, as we shall see.) When a worshipper went into a temple his purpose was to look at the image. Doing so could be a real and moving spiritual experience. If we can combine in our minds the admiration we feel for Greek sculpture and the awe we experience in a great cathedral, we may be able to imagine something of what a visit to his temple might have meant to an ancient devotee. The liturgy that was performed in honor of the god did not take place in the temple at all. It normally consisted of sacrifices offered to the god at altars in front of the temple. Since these sacrifices often involved slaughtering animals and burning parts of them, it was to everyone's advantage that they be held out of doors. These sacrifices were largely the business of the professional functionaries who offered them and were seldom attended by the pagan-in-the-street. Yet it is not proper to refer to all of these worshippers as pagans. The same description would apply for the most part to the Temple at Jerusalem and the sacrifices of our religious ancestors, the Jews. The main difference was that the throne on which the image was placed in pagan temples was vacant in the Temple of Jerusalem. Jews worshipped the invisible and almighty God, the Lord of heaven and earth. But the building, in which there was no image of God, was in other respects much like the temples of Israel's neighbors.

From all this we can readily see that the difference in use between a temple and a church would make a temple of little use as a model for early Christian architecture. Perhaps we need to look for our prototype in that other sort of sacred building used by the Jews, the synagogue. The synagogue, which most scholars date from the time of the Babylonian exile in the sixth century B.C., was a place of worship that required no priest, no sacrifice, nor any cult object. All it required was a *minian*, a quorum of ten adult Jewish males. At the synagogue the main activities in the beginning were reading the Scriptures and commenting on them. Later on, prayer was added to the service. We cannot tell, however, what influence synagogue building may have had on church building; our oldest synagogues seem to date from about the same period as our oldest churches and both display the same architectural form, a form that was just beginning to develop at that time. It is impossible to say which influenced the other if either did. There is a possibility that one synagogue from the first century A.D. has been discovered but we cannot be certain about its identification. This much we can say with certainty: the furnishings of a synagogue would have been quite different from those of a church. The main item of furnishing we associate with later synagogues—the Ark in which the biblical scrolls were stored—was not a permanent fixture in the oldest synagogues. The scrolls were kept in a case that could be moved, and during the services they were brought out and laid in a special place. There was nothing similar to this in early churches. Benches might be placed along the walls of synagogues for people to sit on, with men in one place and women in another. At this time, however, Christians stood for worship and so had no benches. Whatever the relation of the outward form of synagogues to that of churches, then, there is little likelihood that the interior of the synagogue had any great influence on the development of the interior of the church.

The first religious building in which Christians worshipped was the Temple of Jerusalem. We forget all too easily that our Lord and his disciples were Jews who practiced their religion. Yet in the Book of Acts we come across a number of statements like this: "Now Peter and John were going up to the Temple at the hour of prayer, the ninth hour" (3:1). Distinctively Christian worship was being carried on by them at the same time, but they continued to attend the services of the Temple until what must have been fairly near the time of its destruction. St. Paul's arrest was for a supposed violation of Temple law when he went there at the request of the leaders of the church at Jerusalem, and that occurred less than ten years before the Jewish revolt against Rome began. Christians also attended synagogues at times; in most of the cities where he founded churches, St. Paul began his mission in the local synagogue.

The first exclusively Christian worship we hear about, though, takes place in private homes. The Church continued to meet in private homes for some time, but this was not a violation of the principle of sacred space mentioned earlier. According to Eliade, one's home is also a sacred space: "In all traditional cultures, the habitation possesses a sacred aspect" (*The Sacred and the Profane*, p. 53). This is certainly true of the religion of Israel. While the Jews did go to the Temple and to the synagogues, some of their most ancient and characteristic rites took place in the setting of a family meal—the Passover is a case in point. Nor would it be exaggerating to say that among the Jews all meals were holy. Thus the domestic setting of the earliest Christian worship must have seemed entirely natural and appropriate.

The most distinctive act of Christian worship, the Eucharist, was instituted in a private home. Palestinian houses were flat-roofed and usually had stairs going up the outside of the house to the roof so that it could be used as a cool place of withdrawal in the evening, and in the daytime too, if there was some provision for shade. St. Peter, for instance, went to the top of a house in Joppa at about noon in order to pray in the episode described in Acts 10:9. Even poorer families erected awnings, and those who were a bit more comfortable constructed permanent enclosures on their roofs. These rooms were called "upper rooms." Because of their removal from the rest of the house they furnished a protection from interruption desirable for religious devotions. Thus such a room was a convenient place for our Lord to sup with his disciples on the night in which he was betrayed; they, in turn, were engaged in prayer there when he appeared to them after his resurrection.

There are a number of places in the New Testament that tell of churches which met at the home of one of the members. Very likely it was in the upper rooms of these houses that the sacred assemblies were held. If any member of the congregation were a little more wealthy than the others, his house would offer the most spacious accommodations. The apostolic church in Jerusalem met at least occasionally in one such house, that of the mother of John Mark. The reference to this house in Acts 12:12–16 suggests a house built around a courtyard (unlike the one-room dwellings that housed the poorer families—and their livestock) which had an outside gate and an upper room capable of accommodating a congregation that is described as "many." Such a house may have furnished the place of worship for a number of the earliest Christian congregations.

Not all of the assemblies in the primitive Church were in private houses. When St. Paul visited the congregation at Troas and talked with its members until midnight, a young man dozed off and fell out of a third story window (Acts 20:9). Basil Minchin has suggested that this building must have been either a tenement or a warehouse and has demonstrated that some of our earliest churches show that they had been begun in warehouse lofts or rooms above stores (*Outward and Visible*, p. 20). In Acts 19:9 we are told that St. Paul, while in Ephesus, "argued daily in the hall of Tyrannus." The Greek word translated *hall* may refer to the lecture room in the sort of institution that had begun as a military training center, had developed into an athletic institution, and has eventually become the place where young men received both their intellectual and their physical education. We see, then, that the earliest Christians worshipped pretty well where they could.

It has often been suggested that Christians owned no buildings to be used especially for worship until Constantine ended the persecution of the Church by the Edict of Milan in 313 A.D. That very edict, however, proves otherwise. In it we read:

Moreover in regard to the legal position of the Christians we have thought fit to ordain this also, that if any appear to have bought, whether from our exchequer or from any others, the places at which they were used formerly to assemble, concerning which definite orders have been given before now, and that by a letter issued to your office—that the same be restored to the Christians, setting aside all delay and doubtfulness, without any payment or demand of price (trans. by J. Stevenson in *A New Eusebius,* p. 301).

We also have a letter from Constantine to the proconsul of Africa which lists as kinds of property to be restored to Christians "gardens, or buildings or whatever belonged to these churches." There is other evidence in abundance that Christians owned churches before Constantine. The last and most fierce of the persecutions, that under Diocletian and Galerius, began with the destruction of the church in Nicomedia, their capital city.

The church, situated on rising ground, was within view of the palace and Diocletian and Galerius stood on a watch-tower, disputing long whether it ought to be set on fire. The sentiment of Diocletian prevailed, who was afraid that once so great a blaze had started, some part of the city might be burnt; for there were many large buildings around the church. Then Praetorian Guards came in battle array, with axes and other tools; they let loose everywhere, and in a few hours, levelled that very lofty edifice to the ground (Lactantius, *On the deaths of the persecutors,* 11–13, trans. J. Stevenson, *op. cit.,* p. 285).

Records of raids made on some churches show that they were quite prosperous. Archaeologists have actually discovered a few such churches of this period. One of the most important finds was made quite accidentally. When the British army was operating against the Arabs in 1921, a unit began digging trenches in the ruins of what had been a fairly important agricultural and caravan center in the desert along the Euphrates river (the name of the city was Dura-Europos). While the trenches were being dug some wall paintings came to light that suggested that excavation of the site would produce notable artistic remains. One of the buildings unearthed in the early 1930s was a house church. The house was just inside the city wall and consisted of several rooms built around a central courtyard in which there was a pool of water. Originally built as a private home, the house showed signs of having been used by the Christians as a combination church and apartment for either the caretaker or bishop at first. Later on it was converted entirely for worship and other activities of the congregation. In this later stage a wall was knocked out which permitted two rooms to be turned into a eucharistic hall. Across the court is a room used for the baptistry which had probably been a bathhouse earlier. There are other rooms and a portico that were probably used for meetings, instruction, and *agape* meals. Thus we have the ruins of a church that was destroyed around 256 A.D.

Yet another stage of the evolution of church buildings is seen in Aquileia, at the northernmost tip of the Adriatic. The first building on the site was a house with a floor plan similar to that of the church at Dura but of much more spacious and luxurious dimensions. But this building was not only transformed into a church, it was also added to and eventually replaced. Quite extensive additions were made, possibly at the time of the Diocletianic persecution. Then, after the peace of the Church under Constantine, even more elaborate plans were made, which necessitated the destruction of the original building. Consideration of the eleborate new edifice would take us into the next stage of church architecture. Before considering that stage we must look at the transition to it.

In a justly famous passage Dom Gregory Dix, the accomplished Anglican Benedictine liturgical scholar, enunciated a theory of the origin of the floor plan of Christian churches in the arrangement of the houses of wealthy Romans. These houses, which may be seen at Pompeii and elsewhere, pre-

served as their forecourt the arrangement of ancient Roman
farms; the atrium—the central court around its pool—repre-
sented the yard around the well, and the rooms opening off
the atrium opposite the entrance were a vestigial farmhouse.
According to this theory, the central of these rooms was the
place of honor and, when these courts were used for the
Eucharist, the bishop and his presbyters sat there. A fixed
stone table that stood between the room of honor and the
pool was used for the altar (*Shape of the Liturgy*, pp. 22f.).
The atrium was far too public a place for worship, however,
and Basil Minchin has suggested that the dining room of the
Roman house furnished a better model for the development
of eucharistic accommodations of the early church (*Outward and Visible*, p. 37). Since, unfortunately, we have discovered no large Roman houses of this type that we know
certainly to have been used for Christian worship, we cannot say with confidence that either of these theories is
correct.

The real beginning of church architecture—of designing
and erecting buildings specifically for Christian worship—
occurs after the peace of the Church was inaugurated by
Constantine. Constantine had much more to do with this
development than merely permitting it. He, in fact, launched
it. In his capital city of Constantinople he built Holy Apostles and Holy Peace (*Hagia Eirene*), at Nicomedia Our
Saviour, at Antioch an octagonal church, and in Rome he
built or re-built the Lateran, St. Paul's, St. Peter's, St. Law-
rence, Sts. Peter and Marcellinus, St. Agnes, and Holy Cross.
Near Rome he caused churches to be erected in Ostia, Al-
bano, Capua, and Naples. But his greatest enthusiasm,
blended with that of his mother St. Helena, was the erection
of shrines at the holy places in Palestine. The Church of the
Holy Nativity was built in Bethlehem, and another church
was raised on the Mount of Olives in Jerusalsm. Because the
appearance of three angels to Abraham was regarded as an
appearance of our Lord before his Incarnation, a church

was erected at Mambre, too, where that manifestation of God is said to have occurred. Constantine's greatest devotion, though, appears to have gone into the construction of the Church of the Holy Sepulchre with its shrine of the Resurrection. The letter he wrote the bishop of Jerusalem commanding that it be built has been preserved. In it he says:

It will be well, therefore, for your sagacity to make such arrangements and provision of all things needful for the work, that not only the church itself as a whole may surpass all others whatsoever in beauty, but that the details of the building may be of such a kind that the fairest structure in any city in the empire may be excelled by this (Eusebius, *Life of Constantine* 3. 31, Nicene and Post-Nicene Fathers trans.).

Many of the Constantinian churches were never intended for regular parish worship. They were built to celebrate such divine manifestations or theophanies as events in the life of our Lord or to commemorate the death of martyrs. The architectural setting for the celebration of the Eucharist regularly for a local community of the faithful had a different set of requirements from those appropriate to the architectural reminder of a previous manifestation of God's love for men. The one would require room for liturgical movement, while the other would demand focus on a particular spot. It is not surprising then that from the very beginning there developed two distinctive types of church building, each manifesting its own embodiment of the principles of "sacred space," enunciated by Eliade and discussed above. The eucharistic hall was an "aisled basilica" that provided for divine-human encounter in the regular performance of the Church's liturgy, while the shrine was a "central basilica" that directed attention to the very spot where the power of God had been displayed mightily at a holy time in the past. By visiting this place in devotion the worshipper could be ushered into the sacred sphere which had revealed itself there.

The aisled basilica is a rectangular building having its interior divided into three or five aisles by rows of columns. The side aisles are roofed over by a low, shed-like roof, but the center aisle rises higher. It thus has clerestory walls that rise above the roof line of the side aisles, walls punctuated by windows that supply the illumination of the interior and topped off by a roof covering triangular wooden beams. There was usually a rounded apse set in the back wall and this wall may also have been extended slightly to include transepts. This sort of church became standard in the West and is the ancestor of the Gothic churches of the Middle Ages.

Central basilicas came in an assortment of shapes: square, circular, or polygonal. Like the aisled basilicas they had a central section that rose higher than the area which surrounded it and which consisted of columns or piers up to the height of the aisle roof and a clerestory wall above that to its own roof. As we said above, they focused attention on a single spot and so were appropriate structures for memorials, baptistries, and shrines. When architects learned to provide adequate ceremonial space inside these churches and to furnish them with a horizontal axis, this sort of building became standard for Eastern churches. This development was not completed, however, until the sixth century when Hagia Sophia was built at Constantinople on the orders of Justinian.

There has been a considerable debate about how the basilica was developed. Constantine's architects created a new form of architecture which achieved glory at its first blossoming. The scholarly consensus is that the imperial architects did not so much create new components as arrange them in a new way, a way by which space was ordered in a manner appropriate to Christian worship. The result is evaluated in these terms by William McDonald:

Their monumental churches succeeded brilliantly in marking for a rapidly changing world the essence of the newly freed faith, and they set forth profoundly efficacious solutions to the problems posed for architecture by that faith (*Early Christian and Byzantine Architecture,* p. 17).

We have seen now how we got our church buildings, but they have been left, so to speak, with bare floors. We have said nothing of how the first churches were furnished. When we remember that the first places used for Christian worship were private homes we realize that in the beginning there must have been no distinctive furniture for the liturgy. Things in common use around the house were brought in and served liturgical purposes. The earliest altars were ordinary tables and the first bishop's chairs were chairs that the members of the family sat on at other times. Oddly enough to modern minds, the first piece of church furniture to be permanently installed seems not to have been the altar but the *cathedra,* or chair of the bishop. The church at Dura, for instance, has a pedestal on which the chair must have been set but there is no evidence of a permanently installed table. Perhaps it should be explained that the *cathedra* was behind the altar so that the bishop faced his flock; his sermons were delivered from this chair since the seated position was regarded then as the authoritative one. His presbyters were normally seated in a semicircle around him. At first the altar seems to have been well out in front among the people, although then as later the central space was probably kept clear for liturgical action by low screens that delineated it and which were called *cancelli* from which we derive chancel. Eventually raised platforms were made in the chancel on each side so that the Epistle and Gospel could be read from there. There was no need for a pulpit then for, as we said, the bishop preached from his chair. There was no baptismal font in the eucharistic hall. At first baptisms took place out of doors and then in bathhouses and finally in special buildings or rooms called baptistries which were separated from the main building just as were the bathhouses on which they were modelled. As time went on additional elements were supplied to increase the beauty, dignity, or mysteriousness of the church; these included canopies, screens, and curtains. Mosaics appeared on the walls. And this gives us enough stage setting to permit us to go ahead and discuss the worship that occurred in these churches.

PART II

Our question of origins is crucial in all ecumenical discussion because there is no issue that divides Christian bodies more sharply than the evaluation of early Church history. Was the development of the Church as an institution natural and inevitable or was it all a horrible mistake? Catholic-minded Christians tend to the first opinion and Protestants to the second. The phenomenon at stake is referred to by biblical scholars as "early catholicism." The great German Evangelical scholar, Hans Conzelmann, has said that early catholicism "first appears where the ministry has the quality of communicating salvation, where the working of the spirit and the sacrament are bound up with the ministry" (*An Outline of the Theology of the New Testament*, p. 290). Protestants believe this state to be a fall from the heights of the understanding of the Gospel attained by Paul and John; Catholics consider it to be the working out of the logical implications of Pauline and Johannine thought. In keeping with the concept of "inside history," then, the question of the origin of ministry and sacraments is to be investigated not merely to satisfy curiosity about how current practices got started, but to acquire insight into the basic nature of Christianity. Perhaps we may discover that the disagreement between churches need not be so intense as it has been.

The obvious place to begin our study of the origin of sacraments is with the question asked by the Catechism:* "What meanest thou by this word *Sacrament?*" The answer we want

*The Book of Common Prayer, 1928, p. 581

57

to give, however, is not that made in the Catechism. This is
not to say that the answer in the Catechism is wrong; it is
rather that the current trend in theology emphasizes truths
about the sacraments other than those emphasized by the
Catechism. One of the extraordinary characteristics of truth
is that part of it can be so emphasized to the neglect of the
rest that the shape of truth becomes distorted. Thus the history of Christian doctrine has displayed the movement of a
pendulum. A swing in one direction—itself begun as a cor-
rection—is in turn corrected by a swing in the opposite direction. The controversy over sacraments has been about
whether they actually are means by which we receive the
power of God or whether they are mere symbols. It has now
become clear to most Christians that sacraments not only
symbolize the power of God but also convey the power they
symbolize. While this point was being made, though, it was
necessary to let other truths rest in the background. After
all, one cannot talk about everything at once without talking
nonsense. Theology is a logical discipline and cannot, like
Don Quixote's horse, gallop madly off in all directions.

After the Church had talked so long about the power or
the grace of God conveyed by the sacraments, the impression was left that whenever we receive a sacrament we receive a little dab of grace. The more sacraments we receive
the more power we store up. This grace came almost to be
viewed as a possession, as something that we could control
or manipulate for our own benefit. This, however, is not
sacramental theology but superstition. The power of God
never exists apart from God. God never yields his power to
men to manipulate magically in their own behalf. The power
of God can be used only for the purposes of God. The grace
of God can accomplish only one thing in us and this is to
bind us to God. If we do not wish to be bound closer to God
we have no use for grace and the sacraments will not be of
any use to us. The danger of concentrating on the sacra-

ments as means of grace is that this may cause us to forget
that their real purpose is to turn our hearts to God.

This takes us back to the theological presuppositions mentioned in our first chapter. It will be recalled that we said
that the Church is the community through which we have
interpersonal relation with God; it is the sphere of the divine-human encounter. In this perspective we see what the
function of sacraments is in the Church's life of encounter.
Very briefly, the sacraments are the means by which the
Church manifests and effects its character as encounter. The
sacraments are the ways in which the Church becomes what
it is; they are the way the Church performs those acts which
constitute it as what it is. The sacraments are the means
employed by the community of salvation to enter into interpersonal encounter with God. It is in the sacraments that the
Church manifests itself as Church.

These presuppositions furnish the perspective from which
we need to view the institution of the sacraments. When we
look at the way we got our sacraments we do not wish to regard the sacraments as a number of ways through which we
as individuals get different kinds of grace that become our
personal possessions. Rather, we wish to think of them as
the way the community of salvation performs the functions
which are necessary to its life. This means that they are real
means by which the Church has interpersonal encounter
with God, but there is nothing automatic about the way they
work. This way of describing sacramental efficacy can go a
long way toward removing the barrier between Catholic
and Protestant ideas of the sacraments since it safeguards
the Catholic insistence on the sacraments as channels of
grace and yet takes seriously the Protestant fear of viewing
the sacraments as ways in which man can manipulate God.

5

Sacraments of Initiation

The Church as the community of salvation, as the sphere of the divine-human encounter, has its beginning described in the Book of Acts at the account of Pentecost, the day, ten days after the Ascension, when the Holy Spirit came upon the Apostles and the others gathered with them. It was the presence of the Spirit that constituted them as the community of salvation. The Church, then, is the Spirit-filled community. The rest of the Book of Acts is the story of the expansion of that Spirit-filled community throughout the Mediterranean world. The last words of our Lord to his disciples were instruction for this expansion. He said, "You shall receive power when the Holy Spirit has come upon you and you shall be my witnesses in Jerusalem and in all Judea and Samaria and to the end of the earth" (Acts 1:8). As the story is told of this expansion, progress is marked from stage to stage by reports of groups of people in each new area being initiated into this Spirit-filled community. The way they are initiated is well stated by the English theologian, Charles Davis; he says, "Baptism began as the rite by which others were admitted to membership of the original apostolic community" (*Sacraments of Initiation,* p. 40). Baptism, then, is the way that we become members of the community of salvation.

Before we begin our study of properly Christian initiation we would do well to remember that ours is not the only religion that has provision for the incorporation of new members. As Mircea Eliade said:

All premodern societies (that is, those that lasted in Western
Europe to the end of the Middle Ages, and in the rest of the
world to the first World War) accord primary importance to the
ideology and techniques of initiation (*Birth and Rebirth,* pp.
ix f.).

So persistent, in fact, is the human need which is satisfied in
initiatory rites that "the scenarios of initiation still persist
in many of the acts and gestures of contemporary nonreli-
gious man" (*The Sacred and the Profane,* p. 208). Eliade
has seen the pattern of initiation in such diverse activities as
the soldier's "baptism of fire," psychoanalysis, and the entry
of a man into his vocation. The basic characteristic of initiation is that it enables one to meet the demands of a new
status in life. One is enabled to live this new life by receiving
life anew, by being reborn ritually. Thus to locate a Christian institution in the context of the human religious tem-
perament is not to deprive it of its unique significance. The
Christian claim has never been that the Church's members
experience yearnings foreign to other men; it has rather been
that in Christ all the longings of all men are at last satisfied.
  Even the Christian association of rebirth with water has its
similarity with many primitive religions. It should be stressed
here that the main aspect of water in regard to initiation is
not its cleansing power but its power of giving life. And the
very reason that water can be regarded as life-giving is that
it is first recognized as bringing death; death precedes resurrection. Death to an old life is a necessary precondition to
birth into a new life. Water as the sphere of the death struggle appears in the religions of the ancient Orient, Asia, and
Oceania. It is generally agreed among scholars that the
watery chaos that is personified in the old Babylonian creation story as Tiamat, the enemy of the god Marduk, is rep-
resented in an impersonal way in the book of Genesis as
tehom, the Deep. It is the bringing of this watery chaos into

order which constitutes the beginning of creation in Genesis: "The earth was void and without form, and darkness was upon the face of the *deep*; and the Spirit of God was moving over the face of the waters" (Genesis 1:2; italics mine). Thus God conquered the Deep and created the cosmos, the orderly universe. Out of conflict with the forces of death comes life. This motif, so important in the general history of religions, is part of the background of Christian baptism. "One feature of the Bible's perennial appeal is very relevant here: the Bible uses and develops the basic human symbols common to men of all times" (Charles Davis, *Sacraments of Initiation*, p. 13). Thus it is not surprising that in the Old Testament many of the major events of redemption are closely related to water. We see this not only in the creation story but in that of Noah and the flood, in the Exodus from Egypt when God, in the words of the hymn, "led them with unmoistened foot through the Red Sea waters," and when Joshua led the children of Israel across the Jordan river into the promised land.

With this background it should surprise no one to learn that there were many initiatory rites before Christian baptism that made use of water. There are at least three water rites in the various Jewish religious movements of the time of our Lord which may shed some light on the origins of Christian baptism. The first is what is known as "proselyte baptism." When gentile converts were admitted to Judaism they were baptized to the accompaniment of the reading of the commandments of the Law. Thus the rite appears to have united ritual purification with commitment of life. Certain scholars do not believe that proselyte baptism was practiced early enough to have influenced the development of Christian baptism, but the weight of the evidence seems to suggest that it was.

The community at Qumran that produced the Dead Sea Scrolls had their water rites, although it is by no means certain what they were. It appears, for instance, that they practiced daily ceremonial washings, but whether there was in addition a special water rite for initiation or whether initiation merely allowed one to participate in the daily baths is not clear. Some disagreement also exists about whether the water rites took place in one of the elaborate cisterns that archaelogists have uncovered at Qumran or whether drinking water was always too precious in the Near East for that to have been allowed. In the latter case the purification would have been performed in streams. A special cleansing is provided for the victorious soldiers predicted in the *War Scroll* found at Qumran; it is to take place after the final struggle of the Sons of Light with the Sons of Darkness. In the ordinary purifications there is understood to be no cleansing without purity of life and it may be that the agent of this cleansing is thought to be the Holy Spirit.

He shall be cleansed from all his sins by the spirit of holiness [Holy Spirit?] uniting him to His truth, and his iniquity shall be expiated by the spirit of uprightness and humility. And when his flesh is sprinkled with purifying water and sanctified with cleansing water, it shall be made clean by the humble submission of his soul to all the precepts of God (*Community Rule* iii, trans. G. Vermes).

The third water rite that may lie in the background of Christian baptism is the baptism conferred by John the Baptist. The purpose of this rite was to prepare people for the coming of God's kingly rule that was to be inaugurated by Jesus. The coming of the kingdom or reign of God was expected to bring judgment. The way to prepare for that judgment was to demonstrate one's sorrow for one's sins by being baptized. It was expected that this confession of one's shortcomings and the expression of a desire to be on God's side would elicit forgiveness from God. The person thus forgiven would be allowed a place in the community that God was about to establish through the Messiah whose advent John proclaimed.

While all of these purifications could have been part of the background against which Christian baptism was first understood, it is clear that none of them is so direct a precedent as to furnish a complete explanation of what Christians meant by their rite. The Qumran ritual baths appear to have been a regular way of maintaining ceremonial purity, not a once-and-for-all event. The baptism of proselytes and that by John both were performed just once, but they appear to be more a preparation for an initiation than the initiation itself. In the immediate as well as the remote history of religions, then, we have a general background against which we may place Christian baptism, but we do not have precedents close enough to account for the Christian sacrament in every detail or even in its basic significance. This becomes the more obvious when we recall that Christian baptism was (1) in the name of Jesus and (2) was thought to convey the Holy Spirit. No other rite was either so dependent on the one who inaugurated it or was thought to confer such power.

In the New Testament there are only two passages in which there appears to be a commandment for Christians to baptize made by Jesus himself. One of these, Mark 16:16, is not in our oldest manuscripts of that Gospel and is generally believed to be a later addition and not a genuine saying of Jesus. The other passage is Matthew 28:19: "Go therefore and make disciples of all nations, baptizing them in the name of the Father and of the Son and of the Holy Spirit." Most scholars think that the present form of this verse, with its explicit trinitarian formula, has undergone editing by the early Church and does not go back in precisely this wording to our Lord. The lack of an explicit command from Jesus in the New Testament, however, does not mean at all that he did not institute the sacrament. Baptism is taken for granted as the only way of entering the Church throughout the New Testament and this could hardly have happened without a command from our Lord. Furthermore, as C. F. D. Moule has pointed out: "The whole context of thought attaching to Baptism in the New Testament is clearly enough a reflection of Christ's own ministry" (*Worship in the New Testament,* pp. 47f.).

Oddly enough, though, we have very few stories of baptisms that would permit us to reconstruct the form of the rite at that time. The most complete narrative could hardly describe normal practice since it tells of two men riding in a chariot who stop at some water along the way for one to baptize the other (Acts 8:36–39). Another baptism appears to take place in a jail (Acts 16:33) and yet another may have been in an inn (Acts 10:18). Most frequently, though, it occurred out-of-doors in streams.

We are told little about how the action of baptism was performed, but we are told a great deal about its meaning. It will be remembered that when we were talking about the pattern of initiatory rites in general we said that they serve to prepare those who undergo them for a new status in life by letting them die and be reborn ritually. This hope of world religion was fulfilled in Christ.

Do you know that all of us who have been baptized into Christ Jesus were baptized into his death? We were buried therefore with him by baptism into death, so that as Christ was raised from the dead by the glory of the Father, we too might walk in newness of life (Romans 6: 3–4).

It is not to be thought, however, that this was a private salvation for single individuals. It was into the community of salvation that one was initiated.

For just as the body is one and has many members, and all the members of the body, though many, are one body, so it is with Christ. For by one Spirit we were all baptized into one body—Jews or Greeks, slaves or free—and all were made to drink of one Spirit (1 Corinthians 12:12–13).

The new life into which one was born was the life of the Church, the Body of Christ.

Our first description of baptism outside the New Testament may come from a very early period indeed. Some scholars have dated it as early as 70 A.D. Others, however, have placed it several centuries later and most probably regard it as a product of the second century. It appears in a document known as the *Didache* or *Teaching of the Twelve Apostles*. It is a manual to tell Christians how the various activities of the Church are to be performed and is a very simple work, a little crude and a little naive. After a long passage on the moral life it says:

Now about Baptism: this is how to baptize. Give public instruction on all these points [i.e., the preceding moral teaching], and then baptize in running water, "in the name of the Father and of the Son and of the Holy Spirit." If you do not have running water, baptize in some other. If you cannot in cold, then in warm. If you have neither, then pour water on the head three times "in the name of the Father, Son, and Holy Spirit." Before the Baptism, moreover, the one who baptizes and the one being baptized must fast, and any others who can. And you must tell the one being baptized to fast for one or two days beforehand (*Didache*, 7; trans. Cyril Richardson).

From this we learn that baptism was preceded by a time of instruction, that it normally took place out-of-doors, but that in an emergency other arrangements could be made. These probably included the use of either public baths or a private bathhouse. Under pressure even those were not required. Fasting was a usual part of the preparation for baptism.

We have a very complete description of the baptismal process from about 200 A.D. It tells us that men and women were accepted as prospective members or catechumens for about three years before they were baptized. This period was used to test their firmness of purpose and to give them preliminary instruction. Their immediate preparation took place during Lent. During this time their way of life was examined, the power of the devil over them was repressed, and they were given instruction in the faith of the Church on the basis of the creed. Those who were to be baptized solemnly purified themselves with a bath on Maundy Thursday night and fasted on Good Friday. On Saturday they went to the church where the bishop exorcised them. Then they spent the night in a vigil of prayer. At dawn on Easter the baptismal waters were blessed and the candidates removed their clothing. The public baths of the ancient world prevented nakedness from being as disturbing to people then as it would be to us, but men and women were baptized separately. Infants, however, were baptized first of all. The method of baptism as such was described in the chapter on creeds: the candidate was asked if he believed each of the three articles of the creed. As he acknowledged his assent to each article, water was poured over his head (the depth of our oldest baptistries, which did not exceed about eighteen inches, suggests pouring rather than immersion as the oldest method of indoor baptism; it, in turn, was replaced by immersion later on, but gained the ascendancy again when the baptism of infants became normal). The candidate was anointed with the oil of exorcism before his baptism and the oil of thanksgiving afterwards. Then the bishop laid hands on him in confirmation and the new members of the community of salvation received their first Holy Communion on Easter.

This scheme was threatened before it ever came fully into being. The problem was that members of the community of salvation did not always conduct themselves appropriately, and the question arose in the Church of what should be done about sins committed by Christians after they were baptized. An early post-New Testament Christian writing, the *Shepherd* of Hermas, which was written in the first half of the second century, took the position that one forgiveness after baptism was possible, but only one.

If anyone is tempted by the devil, and sins after that great and holy calling in which the Lord has called his people to everlasting life, he has opportunity to repent but once. But if he should sin frequently after this and then repent, to such a man his repentance will be of no avail; for with difficulty will he live (*Mandates* 4.3).

The way that the Church eventually evolved a machinery for the discipline of its erring members will be discussed when we treat the sacrament of penance. Here, though, we need only to call attention to a by-product of the rigor of that discipline, the postponement of baptism. The delay of full initiation into the Christian community until the tempests of youth were past had become so common by the fourth and fifth century that many of the greatest men in the history of the Church were not baptized until they were well into their adult years, including Sts. Ambrose, Augustine, Basil, Chrysostom, and Gregory Nazianzen. With the passage of time, however, the whole society became Christian and then there was a shift in the other direction; infant baptism became normal.

During all this change of the average age at which one was baptized there was an accompanying change in the way in which baptism was administered. We have already said that the oldest baptistries we have discovered were not deep enough to have permitted immersion. As time went on, though, fonts were deepened to make this possible. The purpose of this change was to make the symbolism of baptism more apparent. The going down into the water was seen to represent burial with Christ, and coming up from it symbolized resurrection with him. With the establishment of infant baptism as the norm in the West the manner of administration changed from dipping the candidate under the water to pouring water over him (though immersion has always been the manner of even infant baptism in the East). The change of method led to a change of symbolical interpretation.

In order to safeguard against (the infant's) dying without the
sacrament, they were baptized privately as soon as possible after
birth, and because of the rigors of northern weather, usually by
pouring a little water over the child's head. The symbolism was
that of washing—a cleansing from original sin—and rebirth into
the body of Christ. The concept of the burial in the water was
lost, and hence the sharing in the redemptive death of Christ fell
into the background (Bonnell Spencer, *Sacrifice of Thanksgiving,* p. 50).

This meant that the essential pattern of initiation was ob-
scured and thus it came to be thought that membership in
the community of salvation was something to be earned by
one's own moral efforts or by the application to oneself of
the virtues of the saints stored up in the treasury of merit.
The Reformation doctrine of justification by faith was an
effort to offset this misunderstanding and went a long way
toward doing so. This doctrine did not achieve its objective
completely, however, because of the failure of the Reformers
to recognize the role of baptism in the economy of salvation,
namely that it is initiation into the community of salvation.
It was the beginning of infant baptism as standard practice that raised the question of confirmation as a separate
sacrament. Many churchmen will undoubtedly be surprised
to learn that it had not been one before. In the Prayer Book
rite for confirmation the passage is read from the eighth
chapter of Acts that tells of apostles from Jerusalem going
down to lay hands on people in Samaria, who had already
been baptized, in order that they might receive the Holy
Spirit. Read in the context of that service, the story sounds
like a report of the same kind of event in the early Church
as that which is taking place in the local parish that day. The
apostle is the equivalent of the bishop and he is going to give
the second stage of Christian initiation to those who have already received the first stage. The particular "confirmation
class" at Samaria were all recent converts and so had been
baptized as adults, but if they had been baptized in infancy

then presumably their confirmation would have taken place when they were adolescents.

The shock comes when one turns over two chapters in the Book of Acts and reads that some people to whom Peter was preaching in Caesarea received the Holy Spirit not only without having apostolic hands laid on them but even before they were baptized. Their reception of the Spirit, in fact, is accepted as justification for their baptism, since they were gentiles and up to this point no one knew if one could become a Christian without first being a Jew (either by birth or as a proselyte). Thus we see that in Acts there is no set pattern of Christian initiation by which one is first baptized and then receives the Holy Spirit through the laying on of hands by an apostle.

To get the proper perspective on all of this we must go back to the beginning of this chapter where we saw that it was the presence of the Spirit in the Church that made it the community of salvation. We said there that the Book of Acts contains the story of the spread of the Spirit-filled community throughout the Mediterranean world. To this must be added the information that in the beginning all Christians were Jews, and it had been assumed at first that Christianity was either a party within Judaism or, at most, true Judaism. At that time Christians still attended services in the Temple at Jerusalem and in synagogues elsewhere. When the Church began to spread into areas into which Judaism was not predominant, though—areas such as Samaria, where there was what was regarded as a heretical form of Judaism, or Caesarea, where there were many gentiles—the issue had to be faced of what to do about those who wished to become Christians directly without going through the normative Judaism of Jerusalem. The two stories in Acts that we have looked at, and a number of others as well, suggest that when Christianity appeared to have spread to a new place, apostles investigated to see if what had appeared there was indeed the Church. The presence of the Spirit-filled community in a new place was revealed in ecstatic manifestations of Spirit-possession, such as speaking in tongues. These evidences of the presence of the Spirit proved that it was indeed the Church that had spread there. Thus what we appear to have in Acts is not the story of the institution of the sacrament of Confirmation, but rather a record of apostolic validation of the manifestation of the Church in new places.

When all of that is said, however, it still must be admitted that in the church of which St. Luke, the author of Acts, was a member, part of the baptismal rite was a laying on of hands that was associated with the Holy Spirit. It was not regarded as a separate sacrament, however, but only as a part of the baptismal rite. St. Luke used that association of the Spirit with the laying on of hands narratively by treating visible outbursts of ecstatic phenomena as the effect of the Spirit and therefore as evidence that the Church had truly appeared in a new place.

The practice of including in the total act of baptism a laying on of hands that was associated with the Holy Spirit led theologians in time to speak of the benefits of this laying on of hands separately from their discussion of the benefits of baptism. In the fourth century we find this being done quite explicitly in both the East and the West. In his *Mystagogic Catecheses* St. Cyril illustrates the custom in Jerusalem just as St. Ambrose furnishes evidence from Milan in his works on the "sacraments" and the "mysteries." Yet there are indications that there is a tendency toward that distinction even earlier. But even Cyril and Ambrose regard Christian initiation as one event: "what a later period practised as two clearly separate sacraments, baptism and confirmation, constituted then a single structure of sacred acts —one single act of initiation, which is called 'baptisma' in the most comprehensive sense of this word" (B. Neunheuser, *Baptism and Confirmation,* p. 133).

By this time, though, the completing act of baptism was no longer clearly identified with the laying on of hands.

Around 200 A.D. the laying on of hands was followed immediately by an anointing with oil that was also associated
with the Holy Spirit. By the time of Cyril of Jerusalem it is
this anointing with oil perfumed with myrrh that is considered to be the final act of Christian initiation. The process
was different in the West. While the laying on of hands was
probably accompanied by an anointing quite early, it was
only in the Middle Ages that anointing rather than the laying on of hands was identified as the "matter" of what was
then regarded as a separate sacrament of confirmation. St.
Thomas Aquinas, for instance, does not mention the laying
on of hands at all.

We cannot be certain that anyone regarded baptism and
confirmation as separate sacraments before Gregory the
Great, who became Pope in 590 A.D. As we said, it was the
beginning of infant baptism as a standard practice that
raised the question of confirmation as a separate sacrament.
Before that, baptism and confirmation were regarded as two
components of initiation into the Church. When infant baptism became the norm, though, the Eastern and Western
Churches reacted differently. In the East the baby was baptized and confirmed at the same time. Complete Christian
initiation was given to the infant. This is the Eastern Orthodox practice to this day. In the West, however, initiation
was broken up into two parts (three, if admission to the
Eucharist is counted, as it normally should be). Baptism was
given to infants and confirmation was administered at the
age of discretion—although opinion has differed sharply
from time to time about what age that is. The Western
practice has been inherited by the Anglican Communion. By
dividing into two distinct rites what was originally done as a
sequence we have raised many unnecessary questions about
the relation of baptism to confirmation that will probably
never be answered and only be settled by the restoration to
the rites of initiation of their original unity.

It is under the heading of sacraments of initiation that we

must consider what had been called "the second baptism of penance and reconciliation." Penance is regarded as initiatory precisely because sin results in "a kind of temporary suspension of the effects of baptism" (Louis Bouyer, *Liturgical Piety*, p. 171). The reason for this is obvious: by sin we turn our backs on God. This is to say that we reject fellowship with him and at the same time and by the same act we reject our place in the community which exists to have fellowship with him. And we can go on to use Fr. Spencer's phrase, "for fellowship read eucharist" (*Sacrifice of Thanksgiving*, p. 59). The sacraments, as we said, are not means by which we are enabled to manipulate the power of God for our own benefit, but are rather the way that the Church has interpersonal encounter with God; to reject that fellowship is to cut ourselves off from communion with him, it is to excommunicate ourselves—in practical results if not in ecclesiastical discipline. Being thus excluded from the fellowship, we need to be re-initiated into it and that is accomplished by penance.

It has often been thought that the New Testament Church lived so much in the ecstatic glow of the events which had brought it into existence that its members lived sinless lives. St. Paul, among others, would have been amazed at such an idea. He had the reality of the life of the churches he had founded to disabuse him of any such highflown notions. He told the Corinthian congregation that the sins practiced by some of their members would shock even the pagans (1 Corinthians 5:1). There are, in fact, constant exhortations in the New Testament directed to Christians and telling them to repent of their sins. This repentance cannot stop short at sorrow for having committed sin; it is to be accompanied by prayer and works of mercy. This does not mean that forgiveness is earned—it never could be. It rather means that sincere penitence will move beyond the emotional level and express itself in action. When sin was serious enough in the

New Testament and was not repented of, the church leaders excluded the sinner from the fellowship. This was done not to damn the person, but rather to permit him to be restored to genuine participation in the fellowship. We do not know from the New Testament, however, the way in which this reconciliation was accomplished.

We do have some information about the way that re-initiation into the Christian fellowship occurred fairly early in the life of the Church. This way was not, as many might expect, private confession and absolution as we know it today. Private confession was not originally accompanied by absolution but was "a therapeutic measure in the direction of souls" (B. Poschmann, *Penance and the Anointing of the Sick*, p. 120). It first became a common thing in the monasteries and spread out from there to pious laymen as a means of improving one's personal spirituality. The first real penitential system of the Church was not private but public, because it was recognized that one of the effects of sin was public—it cut one off from the fellowship of the community. This meant that a sinner's penance began—either on his own initiative or that of others—with confession of his guilt to the bishop and the bishop's excommunication of him. Notice that the penance was public but the confession was private. This excommunication did not mean, though, that the Church thus rejected the sinner completely. Penance was a therapeutic practice that had reconciliation as its goal. The sinner was enrolled in the class of penitents and continued to come to church regularly. This was necessary in order that he might show his desire to be restored to the Church's fellowship. But the ruptured state of his participation in the community was demonstrated by his not being allowed to take part in the entire service; not only was he not allowed to make his communion, he could not even make his offering. In some places penitents were not permitted to remain for the entire service. The special part they did have in the liturgy, however, was a blessing from the bishop that was to help the penitent make good use of the period of his penance so that its eventual fruition could be assured.

At the end of the period of penance, which could last anywhere from a few weeks to many years, the penitent was publicly restored to communion. The withdrawal of excommunication was not merely a legal action on the part of the Church; restoration was accomplished by prayer and the imposition of hands by the bishop. Thus it was by a sacramental act that the penitent was re-initiated into the Body from which his sin and consequent excommunication had removed him.

Having noticed the length of time to which the penance could be extended, we need also to remember that only one penance was thought possible. More frequent sins of a nature serious enough to warrant excommunication were regarded as evidence of bad faith, of a lack of sincerity about one's religion that disqualified one for participation in the fellowship. The frailty of human nature, however, continued to manifest itself and the rule of only one penance did not bring an end to sin in the Church; it rather meant that people waited longer to be reconciled. Reconciliation was in fact often postponed until either old age or ill health indicated that drastic action was called for. As we have already seen, other people were even more "careful" and postponed baptism indefinitely. In the early days, however, it is very likely that the great majority of Christians did not ever have to undergo the penitential discipline. Later, the rise of religious orders made it possible for monastic vows to be regarded as a kind of penitential discipline. By this time the need for reconciliation was common enough so that those who underwent public penance were regarded as being not more sinful than their fellow Christians but more virtuous. From that time on, private penance began to replace public penance as the means by which sinning Christians were restored to the community of salvation.

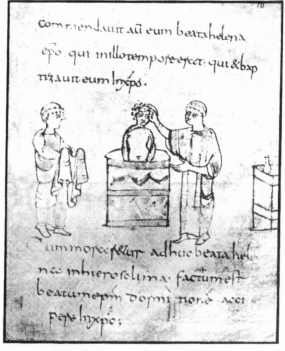

A bishop baptizes an adult in Jerusalem.
From a ninth- century book.

6

The Holy Eucharist

A fact that is surprisingly unfamiliar to most American Christians is that the sites of the crucifixion and resurrection of Jesus are not only known with a fair degree of certainty but are covered by the roof of one church. The church building there now was erected by the Crusaders and it replaced one that was built at the order of Constantine, the first Christian emperor of Rome, and dedicated in 335 A.D. Ironically, the location had been preserved by the Roman emperor Hadrian, who had raised up a pagan temple on the spot 200 years earlier to desecrate the Christian shrine and cause it to sink into oblivion. The only major argument that has been offered against the authenticity of the site has been the assertion that its location was not outside the city of Jerusalem at the time of the execution of Jesus when we know that the crucifixion was outside the city. Summing up the results of recent excavation, however, the great archaeologist Kathleen Kenyon says, "The evidence is thus clear that the traditional sites of Golgotha and the Holy Sepulchre *can* be authentic, but not of course that they *are* authentic" (*Jerusalem: Excavating 3000 Years of History,* p. 154). That is as far as the archaeological evidence can take us, but Miss Kenyon herself goes on to infer that, while the area was outside the city in the time of Jesus, it was inside it in the time of Constantine, and that people then would have had the same difficulty that people today have in accepting the site as genuine had there not been a strong tradition in its favor. Thus the identification is very probably right.

In addition to the Rock of Golgotha on which the cross of Jesus stood and the tomb of Joseph of Arimathea into which the corpse of Jesus was placed and from which he arose, the Church of the Holy Sepulchre has a nave and sanctuary that serve as the cathedral of the Greek Patriarch of Jerusalem, an underground cave where, according to legend, Constantine's mother, Queen Helena, found the cross of Jesus, and a number of chapels scattered around its rather amorphous precincts. Both the Greek Orthodox and the Roman Catholics have chapels over the stone of Golgotha; Coptic Christians from Egypt have a tiny chapel at the back of the tomb itself; the main part of the church, as we said, belongs to the Greek Orthodox; the chapel of St. Helena, on the way down to the cave, is used by the Armenians; and the Roman Catholics have the chapel of the Holy Cross in the cave. Elsewhere, Syrians conduct their services. The only part of the church now available to the poor black monks from Ethiopia is on the roof. The Patriarch of Jerusalem has set aside for the use of Anglicans a chapel in the Greek convent that flanks the entrance to the church. Less than 500 feet south of the Church of the Holy Sepulchre is the Lutheran Church of the Redeemer, built on the ruins of a medieval church. More conservative or fundamentalist groups do not accept the Holy Sepulchre as authentic, preferring to this "Catholic" shrine a site outside the walls of the Old City of Jerusalem discovered in the middle of the last century and given notoriety by the hero of Khartoum, Gen. Charles G. "Chinese" Gordon.

The convergence of all these varieties of Christians around one spot while retaining for themselves separate altars at that spot demonstrates dramatically the importance of the eucharist in the Church. It is in the eucharist that the Church, the community of salvation, experiences that divine-human encounter which is salvation. The refusal of Christians to share in eucharistic fellowship is a denial that they share a common future in God. To be in the Church and to anticipate salvation is precisely what is meant by participating in the eucharist. The eucharist is thus the Church's most characteristic action and at the same time the most effective barrier to real encounter between people who profess the same faith. At the Church of the Holy Sepulchre there is a punctilious care that every variety of Christian be able to have the eucharist, and at the same time that none of them have it together. This anomaly demonstrates the need for Christians to know about the institution of the eucharist by Jesus, what background for it there was in Judaism, and how the Church has come to understand it.

It should surprise no one that the central act of Christian worship is a sacred meal; most religions have one. The majority of the many different cultic acts that are lumped together in the category of sacrifices, in fact, are sacred meals. One of the most convenient distinctions that can be drawn among sacred meals is based on who consumes the food. Some sacrifices are thought to feed only the god to whom they are offered. The food is burned over a fire or is in some other way placed exclusively at the god's disposal. These gift offerings may be made for a number of different motives: they may be offered in gratitude for the gifts of the god's bounty, or they may be given on a tit-for-tat basis, what in Latin is called the principle of *do ut des* (I give so that you will give). There are also sacrifices given with the understanding that the deity depends on the food thus offered to him for his own nourishment and, of course, it is in the best interests of his people that they keep him in condition to be able to assist them.

Another sort of sacrifice provides for part of the offering to be consumed by the god and the rest of it to be eaten by those who offered it. The idea lying behind this is that a shared meal establishes a particularly intimate bond between those who participate in it; this then is a way that communion is built up between a god and his people. A variation on this theme is the sort of meal in which the worshippers eat a kind of food that is thought to represent the deity, their totem animal, for instance, in order to partake of his strength and power. Another sort of sacrifice does not require that the animal be eaten at all; it may be merely driven away. This is expiatory or substitutionary sacrifice by which the guilt of the individual or community is transferred to the animal with the result that the offerer of the sacrifice is exculpated.

All three types of sacrifice—gift, communion, and expiation—were practiced in Old Testament times. In the gift offering, the idea of food for the gods seems pretty well to have been replaced by gratitude to the God of Israel for the deliverance of his people. We see this very clearly in the account given in Deuteronomy of the institution of the offering of the first fruits by which the first and best part of each year's crop is given to God in gratitude for the harvest. When the priest takes the basket with the offering from the worshipper and places it before the altar of God, the one making the offering is required to recite a formula in which he acknowledges that God brought his ancestors out of bondage in Egypt and into "a land flowing with milk and honey" (Deuteronomy 26:6–10).

In the religion of Israel there was also a kind of sacrifice called a *shelem;* since this word comes from the same root as the word for peace, the sacrifice has been called a peace-offering. It was very likely intended to express the fellowship that existed between God and his people. The directions in Leviticus 3 for the offering of the *shelem* tell us that the priests are to offer on the fire the fat covering the entrails, and all the fat on them, the kidneys and the fat on them, and the liver. Nothing is said, however, about what is done with the rest of the animal—all of the best parts according to modern taste. Modern taste, though, ignores ancient psychology; the parts that are offered to God by burning are regarded as the vital centers of the animal, its most important parts and, therefore, those that are most appropriately given to God. But we know from other sources that the rest of the meat was eaten by the offerer and his guests outside the sanctuary and that this meal was considered the essential part of the peace-offering. H. Ringgren, a noted Old Testament scholar of the Scandinavian school, which specialized in studying the worship of Israel, offers an interpretation of this sort of sacrifice: "It is probable that the sacrificial meal was understood as establishing communion between God and the partakers, much in the same way as those who share in an ordinary meal are bound together in an intimate fellowship" (*Sacrifice in the Bible*, p. 25).

To understand the third kind of sacrifice in the Old Testament, expiatory sacrifice, we need to be familiar with the ancient belief about sin. Sin was thought to be any disruption of the order of God's creation, whether it was committed willfully or not. God's order had to be restored in either case and the one responsible had to be reconciled to God. There had to be atonement or, according to its derivation as explained by the *Oxford Universal Dictionary*, at-one-ment. In the history of religions there are two aspects of atonement: propitiation and expiation. Propitiation, or appeasing the anger of God, is rare in the Old Testament. Expiation, which is concerned with the removal of guilt, is far more common. Since sin was thought to be a disruption of God's order, its disastrous results were regarded as inevitable, and so punishment was inescapable. The only way the sinner could avoid the results of his act was to have them fall on someone or something else. The sacrificial way of arranging this was to transfer the guilt of a person to an animal. In the Israelite religion we see this most clearly on *Yom Kippur*, the Day of Atonement, when the sins of Israel were laid upon the scapegoat (Leviticus 16:20–22).

While on first hearing, this may seem a very artificial way of dealing with the problem of human guilt, there is a profound religious insight behind it. The point is not that man can perform some mechanical act and merit God's forgiveness. Any provision for atonement has to be made by God. As Ringgren has said: "Atonement means that God breaks through the connection that exists between sin and guilt, or between sin and its disastrous consequences" (*Sacrifice in the Bible*, p. 38). When Israel offered the scapegoat, she did not expect to earn God's forgiveness but rather to take advantage of the provision for atonement that he had made.

We have spent this much time with the sacred meal and other sacrifices of the past because they delineate some of the main motifs of our own religion. Christians, too, wish to offer expressions of their gratitude to God for all that he has done for them, they wish to enter into fellowship with him, and—when that fellowship has been broken by sin—they wish that communion to be restored through atonement. Indeed, all three of these themes are present in the sacred meal of the Christians. One of its most ancient names is *eucharistia*—the thanksgiving. Now it is often called the Holy Communion. And one of the Gospel accounts of its institution by our Lord has him interpret it in terms of atonement: "This is my blood of the new covenant which is poured out for many for the forgiveness of sins" (Matthew 26:28). The primary reference of the eucharist to Old Testament religion, however, is not in any of these but in another ancient feast—the Passover.

The origin of Passover (*pesakh*) is lost in remote antiquity. Whether the theory of some scholars is correct, that it originated as a festival for the protection of the flocks when the Israelites were nomads, is impossible to determine. In the Old Testament it is treated solely as a commemoration of the deliverance of the children of Israel from bondage in Egypt. In New Testament times it was a pilgrim feast to which as many as 100,000 Jews may have come from all over the civilized world of that period. The head of a family or "company" of at least ten persons would procure a lamb for the feast and a room in which the meal could be eaten. At three o'clock in the afternoon all of the priests of the temple were on duty and the lambs were brought there to be slain. The blood was tossed against the altar and the fat burned; then the rest of the dressed animal was taken to be roasted. That evening it was served to the family or company at a solemn banquet at which wine was drunk, bitter herbs eaten, and the lamb consumed in its entirety. During the meal the "son" asked what made that night different from other nights and he was answered with the story of the delivery of Israel out of Egypt. Then there followed the week-long festival of unleavened bread (*mazzoth*) with which it had long been joined.

Since no part of the lamb was offered to God, there is a sense in which the meal was not a sacrifice at all but rather a symbolical way of repeating the events by which Israel was established as a nation. As Ringgren says:

This places the Passover in a category of religious rituals that aim at the re-enactment in symbolical form of some basic event, the abiding results of which are visibly present, and even reinforced by the rites (*Sacrifice in the Bible*, p. 48f.).

If one were to wonder why the "abiding results" of the past event are "visibly present" through the ritual re-enactment of the event, he would be told by Eliade that this is a fairly common feature of world religions.

Insofar as an act (or an object) acquires a certain reality through the repetition of certain paradigmatic gestures, and acquires it through that alone, there is an implicit abolition of profane time, of duration, of "history"; and he who reproduces the exemplary gesture thus finds himself transported into the mythical epoch in which its revelation took place (*Cosmos and History*, p. 35).

The difference between primitive religion and the Judaeo-Christian tradition in this regard is that our re-enactment is not expected to take us back to some mythological period before history but rather to the moment in history when God revealed himself to his people in a real, historical event.

Or, as Ringgren says: "That which happened once and has a basic significance to the religious community is still present in its results, and its commemoration renews these results in the faith of the worshippers" (p. 50). Thus, the form of the Passover seder as it is still used says that a man ought to think of himself as though he personally had been brought out of Egypt, since the Exodus was as much his redemption as it was that of his forefathers. The commemoration every Passover of God's deliverance of Israel from bondage in Egypt renewed the significance of that event of the past and gave it meaning for each new generation of Jews.

By the time of Jesus the Passover had acquired an additional meaning. Not only was God's redemptive activity in the past commemorated and renewed, but also his decisive intervention in human affairs in the future on Israel's behalf was eagerly and even joyously anticipated. For all but about eighty of the previous 600 years Israel had not been an independent nation but rather had been a part of the empire of whatever world conqueror happened to be around at the time. Sometimes the yoke of captivity was light, but at other times it was gallingly oppressive. Israel was too tiny a nation to hope for deliverance by military might; any hope she had depended upon the intervention into history of the God who had chosen Israel as his own people. The thought about this intervention (which is called *apocalyptic* because of its expression in writings that were regarded as revelations and *eschatological* because it expected the end of the present historical era) centered around a war to the death between the forces of good and evil, both human and supernatural. In some versions of this thought, the forces of good, who would bring to an end the present evil age and usher in the age to come in which the rule of God would dominate history, were thought to be led by an agent of God who was called his "anointed" or Messiah. In our Lord's day, this eschatological hope came to be associated with Passover; many expected that the Messiah would come on Passover to

An ivory pyx used to hold eucharistic Bread. The figures in relief around the pyx represent the miracle of the multiplication of loaves and fishes. Christ is seen in the center. The pyx dates from about the sixth century. (Metropolitan Museum of Art. Gift of J. Pierpont Morgan, 1917.)

set up the kingdom of God. In fact, a number of the revolts
against Rome that broke out at this time, revolts that were
not merely patriotic but also fanatically religious, were begun on the feast of the Passover. So by Jesus' time, pious
Jews at Passover not only looked back to God's deliverance
of Israel in the past but also looked forward to his deliverance of them again in the future.

Now we have all the necessary ingredients for talking
about what Jesus meant by his institution of the eucharist.
Although he appears to have avoided using the term Messiah
as a designation of himself, preferring instead the more
ambiguous label of Son of Man, it was obvious that he considered himself to be God's agent for bringing the present
evil age to an end and inaugurating the reign of God. Possibly one of the reasons he avoided the word Messiah was
that it had come to have political overtones and he did not
see his mission as leading a revolution against Rome. Instead
he focused his efforts on calling Israel to submit to the rule
of the Father. There was an urgency about his preaching because he saw himself in a race against time; the opportunity
for Israel to repent would not be held open indefinitely. By
the time that Jesus got to Jerusalem and the night of the
Last Supper arrived, he knew that Israel would not accept
the proffered invitation. God's rule would have to be inaugurated in another way that would involve his death.

We can imagine the poignancy of his feeling as he came
to this Passover meal. An extraordinary amount of ink has
been wasted over the question of whether the meal was on
Passover night or not. A society in which stores decorate for
Christmas before Thanksgiving should not need Jeremias'
reminder that "the Last Supper would still be surrounded by
the atmosphere of the Passover even if it should have occurred on the evening before the feast" (*The Eucharistic
Words of Jesus,* p. 88). The deliverance which Israel had
looked forward to was now at hand; the Messiah was coming
at Passover. And yet his coming was not the end but a new

beginning. In the future what he did at this time, both at the supper and in his death, would be looked back on as a deliverance more important than the Exodus from Egypt. Future Passovers would commemorate and renew the effects of his death rather than the escape from captivity in Egypt. But these new Passovers, like the old ones, would have a future reference as well as a past one. They would anticipate his return, his second coming, his *parousia*, as it came to be called in Greek.

At this point we must raise the question of whether, to use terms that Jesus would never have thought of, he intended to institute a sacrament or not. Did Jesus know at the Last Supper that history would go on indefinitely and that a church organized in his name would repeat that supper that he celebrated as its most characteristic action, or did he instead think that the time between his death and his *parousia* at the end of the world would be of insignificant duration? It is impossible to be certain. The most that we can be sure about is that he expected his closest followers to continue to eat meals together for a while, at least as they had eaten them with him in the past. When they did so, they would experience his presence with them and would understand those meals in the light of his actions that night and his death the next day. Thus the meals would have something of the sacred character of all Jewish meals and something of the nature of the Passover by recalling and renewing the deliverance he had given them in his death and by anticipating the renewed fellowship with him when he returned at the end. In the Christian Passover the Crucifixion replaced the Exodus as the event to be commemorated, and the return of Jesus came to be the future salvation that was awaited.

One other point needs to be made. Something of the glorious future in store had already been enjoyed during the ministry of Jesus in the meals that he shared with sinners. His table fellowship with tax-collectors, prostitutes, and other outcasts of society was one of the biggest scandals he caused among the respectable people who opposed him. Yet those sinners to whom he opened this fellowship experienced it as the forgiveness of God (already present in history) and an anticipation of the kingdom of God. Thus his ordinary meals before the Last Supper were already eschatological meals in which the reign of God was made present by anticipation. After his death those to whom he had brought forgiveness continued to know this eschatological joy in the eucharist. Thus all the functions of the Jewish system of sacrifice—thank offering, communion, forgiveness, commemoration and renewal of deliverance in the past, and anticipation of consummation in the future—are blended together in the Christian eucharist.

When we move from thinking about the institution of the eucharist by Jesus to the celebration of it by his followers after the Ascension, we are confronted with difficulties of vocabulary. The term "breaking of bread" is used in the Book of Acts in a way that appears to have sacramental overtones, although it is a little hard to see how it could be a designation of the eucharist: "And day by day, attending the Temple together and breaking bread in their homes they partook of food with glad and generous hearts" (2:46). This difficulty is somewhat resolved, though, in the realization that for the Jews there were no meals that were not sacred meals. Undoubtedly at these meals there was some recollection of the saving work of Christ made in the blessing of the food. The reference to attending services at the Temple in the passage from Acts quoted above suggests a possible interpretation of the scant evidence we have. As long as the Church remained in Jerusalem and participated in the Temple services, special attention would have been paid to the Sabbath, which was also a holiday from work and thus a day of rest. We also know from several New Testament references that Sunday, the day of the resurrection, was kept by the Christians as their own holy day. In Acts 20:7 we read: "On the first day of the week, when we were gathered to break bread . . ." It is thus possible that the Jerusalem Christians attended the evening sacrifice at the Temple on the Sabbath. The Sabbath was then over at sundown and the "Lord's Day" begun. Christians would then assemble for their own services, including a eucharist at a meal in the manner of the Last Supper, lasting at times until quite late. Possibly a distinction was made between these great weekly breakings of bread and the daily meals which also had a sacramental orientation, or it may have been that no distinction was made and all breaking of bread was regarded alike; we have too little evidence to be certain. We do know that the expectation of that earliest Christian community in Jerusalem that their Lord would return to them immediately caused them to be an extraordinarily coherent body that spent much time together.

The only celebration of the eucharist in the New Testament of which we are given any detail, however, was not in Jerusalem and was also not a model to be emulated. St. Paul wrote to the church at Corinth condemning it for its sacrilegious manner of thanksgiving:

When you meet together it is not the Lord's supper that you eat. For in eating, each one goes ahead with his own meal, and one is hungry and another is drunk. What! Do you not have houses to eat and drink in? Or do you despise the church of God and humiliate those who have nothing? . . . So then, my brethren, when you come together to eat, wait for one another—if anyone is hungry, let him eat at home—lest you come together to be condemned (1 Corinthians 11:20–22, 33–34).

It is obvious from this that the eucharist continued to be celebrated in conjunction with a meal, even in gentile territory. It is even possible that the excesses committed at Corinth were analogous to those of certain pagan cultic meals. No hint is given here of frequency of celebration, but the lack of a Temple to relate to and of the sort of communal

living arrangement that the Jerusalem church apparently
had at first, together with perhaps a diminished expectation
of the Lord's immediate second coming, may have caused
Christian assemblies to meet less frequently than the daily
worship of the Jerusalem church.

There is some question of exactly when the sacrament became separated from the supper. The fact that all common
meals would have had a sacred aspect prevents our discerning the precise degree of sacredness that was attached to
each of the meals that we have record of. Our earliest evidence is ambiguous in the extreme; a case in point is *Didache*
9–10:

Now concerning the giving of thanks. Give thanks in the following manner.
First, concerning the cup:
   We thank you, our Father, for the holy vine of David your
   servant which you have made known to us through Jesus
   Christ your Servant. Glory to you forever!
And concerning the broken loaf:
   We thank you, our Father, for the life and knowledge which
   you have made known to us through Jesus your Servant. Glory
   to you forever! Just as this loaf previously was scattered on the
   mountains, and when it was gathered together it became a
   unity,
   So may your Church be gathered together from the ends of the
   earth into your kingdom.
   For glory and power are yours forever, through Jesus Christ!
But let no one eat from your Eucharist except those who are baptized in the Lord's name. For the Lord also has spoken concerning this:
   Do not give what is holy to dogs.

Several features of this rite make it very dubious that it is
for the celebration of the eucharist, features such as blessing
the cup before the bread, the lack of any memorial (*anamnesis*) of our Lord's saving work, and the absence of any reference to his body and blood. Thus most scholars regard this

as the form to be used for an *agape* or love feast after the
sacrament had been separated from the supper. There certainly is what appears to be a form for a Sunday eucharist
later on in the *Didache*. If this interpretation is correct, then,
the separation of the eucharist from a meal would have occurred before the *Didache* was written. Such a conclusion
does not carry our efforts to date the separation a great deal
farther since the date of the *Didache* and that of its sources
is a matter of vigorous debate. Generally, though, it seems
likely that the *Didache* incorporates material from the late
first and early second centuries but that the present form of
the work was not assumed before the middle of the second
century.

More precise dating of the separation can be based on a
letter written around 112 A.D. to the emperor Trajan by
Pliny, the governor of the Roman province of Bithynia. Pliny
says that the Christians met on a certain day before sunup
and, as the Latin appears to say, "bound themselves with an
oath." But the Latin word which is translated "oath" is *sacra-
mentum*, which may mean that they celebrated the sacrament in the morning. At any rate, Pliny says that they met
again for "ordinary and harmless food," which could have
been an evening *agape* after a morning eucharist at which
there was no meal.

Our next evidence comes to us from just after 150 A.D.;
Justin Martyr, one of the first Christian writers to make a defense of the faith to the pagan world, described the worship
of the Church of his time in his first *Apology*. He mentions
two occasions for the celebration of the eucharist. One is defi-
nitely the climax of an annual Baptism-Eucharist such as
some writers think existed as early as the *Didache* and the
other is an ordinary Sunday celebration. The worship is described as follows:

And on the day called Sunday there is a meeting in one place of
those who live in the cities or the country, and the memoirs of

the apostles or the writings of the prophets are read as long as time permits. When the reader has finished, the president in a discourse urges and invites us to the imitation of these noble things. Then we all stand together and offer prayers. And, as said before, when we have finished the prayer, bread is brought, and wine and water, and the president similarly sends up prayers and thanksgivings to the best of his ability, and the congregation assents, saying the Amen; the distribution, and the reception of the consecrated (elements) by each one, takes place and they are sent to the absent by the deacons. Those who prosper and who so wish, contribute, each one as much as he chooses to (1 *Apology* 67; trans. E. R. Hardy).

From this we notice several things: The first is that the regular Sunday eucharist now has a preparation consisting of readings from the Old and New Testaments and a sermon on the readings by the bishop ("president"). This preparation could hardly have fitted into the meal context of the earlier rite. It is, in fact, an adaptation of the standard service of the Jewish synagogue, just as the eucharistic prayer itself, when it came to be written down, also shows marked influence of synagogue prayers.

Other features of the eucharist of Justin are worthy of attention. It begins with the prayer of the faithful in which the faithful themselves participate; these prayers correspond somewhat to the Prayer for the Whole State of Christ's Church in the Book of Common Prayer.* Next follows the offertory of the eucharistic elements, which does not occur until immediately before the prayer of consecration is to be made over them by the bishop. The baptismal form of the eucharistic liturgy, which Justin also describes, tells of the kiss of peace that is exchanged by the faithful after they have completed their prayer. "They affirmed by means of the kiss of peace that they all wanted to be brothers and sisters of one family, because all are children of the Heavenly Father" (J. A. Jungmann, S.J., *The Early Liturgy,* p. 41). A feature which must appear striking to the modern reader

*The Book of Common Prayer, 1928

is that there is no penitential element—nothing of confession or absolution—in this rite. These elements were absent from all of the earliest rites for the eucharist because grievous sin was treated with a heavy penitential discipline that did not allow the penitent to receive communion or even to make his offering, as we saw in the previous chapter. Less serious sins were not confessed or absolved until the rise of the monastic orders.

The prayer of consecration or canon in the liturgy described by Justin was prayed extemporaneously by the bishop (who was the usual celebrant of the eucharist at the time). Within half a century, however, a consecration prayer was written down and has been preserved. The consecration could still be prayed extemporaneously but at least the possibility of a more fixed form was held out. Hippolytus, who wrote the prayer, said: "It is not, to be sure, necessary for anyone to recite the exact words that we have prescribed, by learning to say them by heart in his thanksgiving to God; but let each one pray according to his ability" (*Apostolic Tradition* 10.4, trans. B. S. Easton).

We are fortunate to have any form from so early a time, even if it was not a required form; it tells us much about how the eucharist was celebrated at that time. The rite, which is short, bears quoting in full. The form given is for a bishop's first eucharist after his consecration and the consecration itself is the only preparation, just as baptism was the preparation in Justin's initiatory eucharist, rather than a service of the Word based on the synagogue worship.

And when he is made bishop, all shall offer him the kiss of peace, for he has been made worthy. To him then the deacons shall bring the offering, and he, laying his hand upon it, with all the presbytery, shall say as the thanksgiving:

The Lord be with you.

And all shall say

> *And with thy spirit.*
> Lift up your hearts.
> *We lift them up unto the Lord.*
> Let us give thanks to the Lord.
> *It is meet and right.*

And then he shall proceed immediately:

We give thee thanks, O God, through thy beloved Servant Jesus Christ, whom at the end of time thou didst send to us a Saviour and Redeemer and the Messenger of thy counsel. Who is thy Word, inseparable from thee; through whom thou didst make all things and in whom thou art well pleased. Whom thou didst send from heaven into the womb of the Virgin, and who, dwelling within her, was made flesh and was manifested as thy Son, being born of (the) Holy Spirit and the Virgin. Who, fulfilling thy will, and winning for himself a holy people, spread out his hands when he came to suffer, that by his death he might set free them who believed on thee. Who, when he was betrayed to his willing death, that he might bring to nought death, and break the bonds of the devil, and tread hell under foot, and give light to the righteous, and set up a boundary post, and manifest his resurrection, taking bread and giving thanks to thee said: Take, eat: This is my body, which is broken for you. And likewise also the cup, saying: This is my blood, which is shed for you. As often as ye perform this, perform my memorial.

Having in memory, therefore, his death and resurrection, we offer to thee the bread and cup, yielding thee thanks, because thou hast counted us worthy to stand before thee and minister to thee.

And we pray thee that thou wouldest send thy Holy Spirit upon the offerings of thy holy church; that thou, gathering them into one, wouldest grant to all thy saints who partake to be filled with (the) Holy Spirit, that their faith may be confirmed in truth, that we may praise and glorify thee. Through thy Servant Jesus Christ, through whom be to thee glory and honor, with (the) Holy Spirit in the holy church, both now and always and world without end. Amen (*Apostolic Tradition* 4).

We notice a number of things immediately. The presbyters —from the Greek word *presbyteros* from which is derived our English word "priest" but which is translated "elder"— seem to share in the task of offering the thanksgiving with the bishop. The connection with a meal seems almost completely to have disappeared, although a vestige remains in the provision for the bishop to bless olive oil, cheese, or olives at the time of the offertory. Directions for holding an *agape* meal are given in an entirely different part of the book (chap. 26).

Perhaps the most striking aspect of this rite is the brevity of it. There is not even a provision for the prayer of the faithful with its intercessions for the living and the dead (although it is possible that such a prayer was said at a regular Sunday eucharist). And modern ears that hear "Lift up your hearts" but no "Holy, holy, holy" may have a sense of waiting for the other shoe to drop. But, even though this is one continuous prayer and not a number of short ones as Jewish forms were, many Jewish elements remain, such as the thanksgiving for creation and redemption and a memorial (*anamnesis*) of the saving work of God (although here in the Christian form of a remembrance of the mighty acts of Jesus). In line with later forms of Christian eucharistic prayer there is also the account of the institution of the sacrament by Jesus and an invocation of the Holy Spirit (*epiclesis*). So complete is this first prayer of consecration of which we have a copy that the distinguished German liturgical scholar, Theodor Klauser, has said: "The eucharistic prayer, as those who read it will have sensed, was, in essence, then exactly what it is today" (*A Short History of the Western Liturgy*, p. 17).

The liturgy would develop in different ways in different places. Historians of the liturgy speak of great "families" of forms that developed in one place or another: East Syrian, West Syrian, Alexandrian, Roman, and Gallican. From these developed the Roman rite that was used through the Middle

Ages to the present and was the basis for the Prayer Book liturgy. From them developed also the classical forms of the Byzantine eucharist, the liturgies of St. Basil and St. John Chrysostom, which are still used by the Eastern Orthodox. But all of the necessary ingredients for a eucharistic rite are already present in this liturgy of St. Hippolytus, which we have looked at. This ancient rite stands between the sacred meals of the Jews and our own way of offering eucharist today, reminding us of our fellowship with all the generations of the people of God. Such a reminder can cause us to end where we began—with the diversity of rites offered at the Church of the Holy Sepulchre. Having seen how the Church enters into divine-human encounter in the eucharist, we can long for the day when we can give new meaning to the words of the hymn and sing:

> One body we, one Body who partake
>   One Church united in communion blest;
> One name we bear, one Bread of life we break,
>   With all thy saints on earth and saints at rest.
>
> One with each other, Lord, for one in thee,
>   Who art our Saviour and one living Head;
> Then open thou our eyes, that we may see;
>   Be known to us in breaking of the Bread.

7

"Commonly Called Sacraments"

One way you could describe the history of theology is as "the great sacrament counting contest." One entry in the contest appears in the second Office of Instruction in the Prayer Book. In answer to the question, "How many Sacraments hath Christ ordained in his Church?," the response is made: "Christ hath ordained two Sacraments only as generally necessary to salvation; that is to say, Baptism and the Supper of the Lord."* The limit of the number to two, then, is based on (1) the institution of the sacrament by Christ and (2) its reception being reckoned as a prerequisite to salvation for all people (which is what *generally* meant in 1604 when this question was added to the Catechism). We have already seen that there is some question about what it means to say that Jesus instituted a sacrament when it is by no means certain that he expected the world to continue indefinitely. The second half of this definition is equally shaky because very few Christians today believe that only Christians will be saved, much less that only Christians who have received two sacraments will be.

This number of two, however, was set in conscious opposition to the enumeration of seven sacraments by the Roman Catholics. The twenty-fifth of the Articles of Religion in the back of the Prayer Book says:

*Book of Common Prayer, 1928, p. 292

Those five commonly called Sacraments, that is to say, Confirmation, Penance, Orders, Matrimony, and Extreme Unction, are not
to be counted for Sacraments of the Gospel, being such as have
grown partly of the corrupt following of the Apostles, partly are
states of life allowed in the Scriptures. . . .

Catholic-minded Anglicans since at least the last century
have tried to restore the concept of seven sacraments by
pointing out that, while there are only two sacraments generally necessary to salvation and, in that sense, only two
sacraments "of the Gospel," that does not mean that there
are not other "outward and visible sign(s) of an inward and
spiritual grace" that are the "means whereby we receive this
grace"; in other words, this does not mean that there are
not other sacred acts that may be legitimately called sacraments.

As well-intentioned as this effort was, it did overlook the
sacrament-counting nature of the history of theology which
we mentioned. The number of seven had by no means been
universally accepted before the Reformation. Hugh of St.
Victor, for instance, listed as many as thirty, although he
placed five in a privileged category. Others at the same time
said fewer or more, or else chose the same number but dis-
agreed about which constituted the five. It was not until
1150 that Peter Lombard published his *Sentences*, destined
to become the theological textbook of the Middle Ages, and
gave his authority to the number seven. His count was given
ratification officially by the Council of Florence in 1439, only
ninety years before the beginning of the English Reformation.

Indeed, the word *sacrament* is Latin in origin and was
only introduced into the Christian vocabulary by Tertullian
in the early third century when he coined singlehandedly
most of the technical terms for Latin theology. There was no
precise definition of sacrament, however, before St. Augustine gave one in the fifth century. Poschmann is quite cor-

rect when he says that in the early Church "as yet there was no clear concept of a sacrament differentiating individual sacraments from each other and from non-sacramental actions" (*Penance and the Anointing of the Sick*, p. 237). The lateness of such distinctions means that we often have difficulty fitting earlier religious phenomena into the mold of a later neat division of sacred acts into seven sacraments. We can, for instance, point to a lot of times in the early Church when men were anointed with oil for a number of purposes, but to ask upon what occasions those anointings were the sacrament of unction is to raise a question that would never have occurred in the period when the anointings took place. This means that the concept of seven discrete sacraments is not really very helpful as a category for evaluating the sacred acts of the early Church.

A further barrier to any insistence upon the number seven is the theological understanding of the sacraments which we have advanced. As we said, we should not regard sacraments so much as the ways through which we get different kinds of grace as the way the community encounters God. This means that there is a most profound sense in which there are essentially two sacraments and these are not baptism and Eucharist. The two sacraments in the strictest sense of the word are Christ and his Church. It is in Christ and the Church that divine-human encounter occurs absolutely. Thus Schillebeeckx can refer to Christ as "the primordial sacrament" and to the Church as "the earthly sacrament of Christ in heaven" (*Christ the Sacrament*, chs. 1 & 2). But these two essentials sacraments (which are in reality the same one) have *at least* seven ceremonial manifestations and so it is not incorrect in that sense to speak of seven sacraments. For that reason and because it has been customary to think of seven sacred acts as sacraments, we will include at this point a very cursory discussion of the only two which are not treated elsewhere in the book: unction and matrimony.

It might be thought that unction and matrimony are an unfortunate coupling, suggesting perhaps that among the disasters that overtake people and call for divine remedy are disease and marriage. Yet they belong together for a much more profound reason than the mere fact that they are the leftovers, fitting uncomfortably into any other division we have made. What unction and matrimony have so profoundly in common is that they deal with conditions that are by no means limited to Christians; all people get sick and live in families. Disease and marriage, then, belong to nature rather than grace, to use one theological way of putting it. This is what the Articles of Religion referred to in the statement that the five "commonly called sacraments" are "such as have grown partly of the corrupt following of the Apostles, partly are states of life allowed in the Scriptures." Marriage is an allowable state of life, and the Reformers regarded unction as a corrupt following of the Apostles because it was given only *in extremis,* i.e., to the dying as a last rite rather than to the sick for healing. Matrimony and unction, then, are ways that Christians do things that nearly all people do; they are the ways that disease and family life are incorporated into the economy of salvation. They are the ways that Christians deal with the stuff of which everyone's life is made.

Anointing with oil was a treatment of the sick that was common in ancient times among both Jews and gentiles. The good Samaritan, for instance, poured oil and wine on the wounds of the man who fell among thieves (Luke 10:34). In addition to this reliance upon the medicinal properties of olive oil there was also the use of physical media by wonder workers to effect cures. Our Lord himself is reported using such things several times, although we are not told that he employed oil. According to Mark 6:13, however, his disciples did when he sent the Twelve out on their mission to Israel: "And they cast out many demons, and anointed with oil many that were sick and healed them." The scriptural au-

thority for a sacrament of healing, though, is not usually seen
here but in James 5:13–16.

Is any among you suffering? Let him pray. Is any cheerful? Let
him sing praise. Is any among you sick? Let him call for the elders of the church, and let them pray over him, anointing him
with oil in the name of the Lord; and the prayer of faith will save
the sick man, and the Lord will raise him up; and if he has committed sins, he will be forgiven.

It should be noticed that while there is much discussion
of healing in the New Testament, very little of it can be
understood as the practice of a sacrament of healing. Jesus'
healing certainly is not to be seen that way. Nor was it regarded basically as a display of his divine power, as though
he were the supreme example of the category of miracle
workers. Rather his healing activity is to be understood
against the background of his mission to inaugurate a new
age in which the reign of God was effective in history. He
said, "If it is by the finger of God that I cast out demons,
then the kingdom of God has come upon you," (Luke 11:20)
and all the other cures that he performed were also accepted
as evidence of the presence of the kingdom in power. The
healing that the Twelve did during his lifetime was an extension of his own authority; their cures too demonstrated that
new power for good was loose in the world because God's
reign had drawn near. In the early Church the emphasis
seems to have shifted and the ability of an individual to heal
is regarded as a special gift (or, to use the Greek word,
charisma) bestowed upon a particular Christian for the benefit of the whole body of the Church. St. Paul, for instance,
ranks it with miracle working, prophecy, the ability to distinguish between spirits, speaking in tongues, and interpreting tongues as gifts that some Christians receive (1 Corinthians 12:9–10). Yet this change of emphasis should not be
exaggerated; to say that the reign of God had been inaugurated and to say that the Holy Spirit was active in the

Church is to make the same statement in two different ways.

With this in mind when we look at the directions for elders to anoint the sick with oil, the sacramental understanding of healing is moderate even there. Bo Reicke is probably right in saying that here "the healings of Jesus are thought to be perpetuated and effected through the officials of the church, as a result of intercessory prayer confirmed by the use of the holy oil" (*The Epistles of James, Peter, and Jude*, p. 59). Jesus' inauguration of the reign of God made it possible for such cures to take place and, just as Jesus and the Twelve used physical media in some of their healings, so the Christian community of which the author of James was a member used oil. We are not told what interpretation is given the role of the oil in these cures, whether it was thought to be therapeutic in itself in a natural way or whether it was seen as a vehicle of religious power or what, but most likely it was thought of merely as a continuation of the practice of the Twelve.

One thing that is clear is that no evidence we have from the early Church indicates that anyone thought that a sacrament of healing had been instituted for which the matter was oil. This silence of the sources does not mean that anointing was not done or that it was; it means only that we have little information on the subject. But if the practice were widespread, we would expect more reference to the practice to have come down to us than has been preserved. The first Christian who quotes from the passage in James is Origen, who wrote in the early third century, but he interprets the infirmity to be spiritual rather than physical, so that he describes penance rather than unction. The earliest unambiguous reference we have to anointing for healing comes from Pope Innocent I who died in 417. From him we learn that the oil should be blessed by the bishop alone, but that it may be applied by him or by a priest or even a layman. From then on references become more frequent.

The quotation from James not only states that the sick

person would be raised up, but also that if he had committed any sins they would be forgiven him. We also saw that Origen interpreted the basic sense of the passage as penitential. It is small wonder then that in the course of time theologians came to regard unction not so much as a sacrament of healing as the form of penance appropriate to those at the point of death—*in extremis,* as the Latin phrase would have it—and thus the sacrament came to be called extreme unction. In the teaching of the New Testament, healing was obviously considered to be something within the power of God and it appears to have happened often. The caution of Poschmann, however, is relevant:

James cannot possibly have promised recovery unreservedly to all sick believers who obey his directions, as in the long run this would be an assurance of immortality. The suggestion that he wanted to keep all sick people alive until the *Parousia* (i.e., the second coming of Christ) is groundless and quite inconsistent with the ideas of primitive Christianity (*Penance and the Anointing of the Sick,* p. 235).

Yet there is an element of bodily healing that is ineradicable in unction, even though in most of the history of the Church healing has probably been thought of more as the result of the personal charisma of individual Christians than as the efficacious working of a sacrament. Unction, though, as a sacrament, has always been connected with at least a spiritual strengthening, and sometimes with forgiveness as well. That forgiveness should be conveyed with physical healing illustrates the biblical belief that there is often (though not always) a connection between sin and disease.

We have spoken of sacraments as means of divine-human encounter. This element is not lacking from unction. The restoration of the bodies of the members is a restoration of the Body. Unction also recognizes that we must pass through death to achieve resurrection into the Church triumphant. As Bouyer said:

Thus, they are prepared to go through the "way of all flesh," as
the Old Testament phrase expressed it, to everlasting life. By this
means, human infirmity, including human death, is . . . not only
an image of the Mystery, but also to be absorbed into it and to
work toward its final fulfillment (*Liturgical Piety*, p. 175).

   To have said all this is by no means to have said all that is
theologically significant about human disease and suffering,
but is only to have discussed slightly the rite by which disease
has been incorporated into the economy of salvation. By the
same token, in speaking of holy matrimony we will not discuss
all important spiritual truths that Christians have perceived
about marriage, but will again talk only about the history of
the rites by which Christians have signified those percep-
tions. We have no description of a Christian wedding that
comes to us from earlier than the ninth century. Before that
we have indications that Christians had special nuptial cele-
brations of the eucharist and a blessing was given at that
time, but we have no full report. The ninth-century directions come from the consultation of Pope Nicholas I with
the Bulgarians. He tells them that preliminary to the marriage ceremony is the public betrothal of the couple, the
delivery of the ring by the groom to the bride, and the delivery of the wedding contract with its provision for a dowry.
The ceremony includes the nuptial mass, the blessing, and a
coronation of the bride and groom. The striking feature of
this to modern people is that what we would call the wedding proper is described here among the preliminaries. In
point of fact, the entire form is taken over from Roman cus-
toms and the main difference is that Christians offer the
eucharist—the Christian sacrifice—instead of sacrifices to
pagan gods. The exchange of vows, even in the ninth century, was not presided over by a priest; that did not come
until the eleventh century, although we hear as early as 115
that the bishop should give his sanction to the wedding.
   The tardiness of the Church in providing any ceremony

for marriage that was distinctively Christian indicates the lack of sense that there was any essential difference between what Christians did and what pagans did when they got married. The act was the same; the understanding of it was different. Christians fitted marriage into their beliefs about God, his creation of the world, and his purpose for humanity. They saw their marriages in the light of their duties to God and neighbor. As St. Paul indicates in the seventh chapter of 1 Corinthians, they realized that it was better for Christians to marry one another than to marry pagans because husband and wife needed to agree on the nature of marriage. Thus a natural human institution was taken into the economy of salvation and seen in a theological perspective. Christian marriage was like any other marriage except that it was contracted by Christians, who gave their Christian understanding to what they and other people did when they married.

Now, as then, this Christian perspective affects the way that one sees many problems connected with marriage. Some of the most profound questions of our troubled times are related to marriage: the population explosion, abortion, women's rights, divorce, sexual morality, and homosexuality. Since Christians do not believe that they differ from the world in practicing a different kind of marriage, but rather in having a fuller understanding of all marriage, they face these issues with the conviction that their commitments are not only binding on themselves but reflect the true dimensions of these issues. Our investigation of the early development of Christian institutions is not the place to spell out these commitments, but it does show us that Christians, by their incorporation of marriage into the economy of salvation, see this natural institution of marriage in its true supernatural meaning.

The Emperor Justinian and his court. The second figure on Justinian's left is Maximianus, Bishop of Ravenna. He is seen vested in a dalmatic, a wide chasuble of the sort called a phelonion, and a pallium, and is carrying the portable altar cross. One of his two dalmatic-clad deacons carries a book of the Gospels and the other a censer. This is a reproduction of the original mosaic in the Church of San Vitale, Ravenna. (Metropolitan Museum of Art, Fletcher Fund, 1925.)

PART III   8

Evolution
of the Ministry

The question of how we got our ministry may
seem simpler to Anglicans than some of the
others we have investigated. After all, the
preface to the ordination rites in the Book of Common
Prayer says, "It is evident to all men, diligently reading
Holy Scripture and ancient Authors, that from the Apostles'
time there have been these orders of Ministers in Christ's
Church,—Bishops, Priests, and Deacons" (p. 529).* It takes
only a little reflection to realize, however, that it is not evident to all men; the forms of ministry manifested in other
Christian bodies indicate that the matter is not all that simple, straightforward, and obvious. Others have read the evidence in a different way and organized themselves accord-
ingly. Nor can we say that their different interpretation is
merely a result of their not having studied the Holy Scriptures and ancient authors diligently enough. Thus we must
go back over the evidence ourselves to see what picture of
the ministry in the primitive Church emerges. We do not
hope to be more perceptive than our religious forebears, but
we do have much more evidence from the period to work
with than they did.

Before we begin our historical survey we need to make
some preliminary distinctions. First we need to fit the question of ministry into the context of all that we have said
about sacraments. We said that sacraments should not be regarded as a number of ways through which we as individuals

get different kinds of grace that become our personal possessions. They should be thought of, rather, as the way the community of salvation performs the functions that are necessary
to its life. Ordination would thus be the means by which
the community authorizes those officers through whom it
will perform those functions. Those functions all have to do
with the life of the Church as the community of salvation in
which people enter into interpersonal relation with God.
Among these activities through which we have divine-human encounter we think first and foremost of the holy eucharist. There are also those activities through which others are
brought into the community of salvation; among these we
think of evangelism and initiation. Lastly we think of those
activities by means of which the life of the community is
sustained; these include the training of those who already
belong to the community, the administration of the community, the pastoral care of souls, and the like.

It is obvious from this list that not all of the functions of
the Body of Christ are sacramental. Also obvious from our
enumeration of ministerial functions is the fact that ministry
is not the exclusive prerogative or responsibility of the
clergy. Nor can we divide ministry into a sacramental category which is the exclusive domain of the clergy and a non-
sacramental category in which the unordained may function.
Very few of these functions can be performed by the clergy
alone. The eucharistic sacrifice, for instance, is not offered
by the priest in splendid isolation from the congregation; it
must be offered by and for the entire body. Many of these
acts can be performed by the laity, even some that are sacramental. For example, baptism may be conferred by a layman in case of dire emergency. While the clergy do have a
special responsibility to proclaim the faith to those who have
not accepted it, much of the most effective evangelism is
done by laymen and that is as it should be. So ministry is
not the exclusive prerogative and responsibility of the clergy.

That brings us to two cautions: (1) ministry in the Church
is not an occasion for pride but for humility, and (2) minis-

try in the Church is not necessarily professional. The first
of these points is made thoroughly and effectively by the
distinguished Roman Catholic biblical scholar John L. Mc-
Kenzie in his important book, *Authority in the Church*. He
points out that the one sort of analogy which our Lord consistently refused to apply to authority in the Church was that
of secular rule: "You know that those who are supposed to
rule over the gentiles lord it over them, and their great men
exercise authority over them. But it shall not be so among
you; but whoever would be great among you must be your
servant, and whoever would be first among you must be
slave of all" (Mark 10:42–44). The status of an officer in the
Church, then, is the status of a slave. The use that is to be
made of authority in the Church is mission; the authority of
the Church is to proclaim the Gospel and to administer the
sacraments. The authority to do this is a gift of God's Holy
Spirit and not anything that man can give, and the supreme
authorizing gift of the Spirit is that love for all people that
makes one wish to spend himself in the task of bringing them
into the fellowship of redemption. The very word which we
translate *ministry* means "the status of a lackey." Thus, as
McKenzie said, "If (Jesus') followers are to continue the
mission he has given them, they too must conceive of themselves as lackeys and slaves of others" (p. 28).

He commissioned the Church to find new forms and structures
for an entirely new idea in human association—a community of
love (p. 32f.).

Love is the supreme motivation both of the officers and of the
other members of the Church; with this motivation, anything like
a power structure is forever excluded from the Church. Love is
the only power which the New Testament knows (p. 85).

The other caution is that the clergy are not necessarily vo-
cational Church workers, not what Sinclair Lewis called
"professional good men" hired by the rest of us to do good
for us vicariously. Rather, they are organs of the body

through whom the body performs some of its functions. None of these functions, however, requires that it be performed by someone who makes his living that way. In the early Church it appears that the majority of those who held Church office were not employees of the Church, that they made their living doing something else. The point is more important for us today than it has been for many intervening generations because there is now a reappearance of what are called "non-stipendiary" clergy. (Those interested in this movement should read the exciting book, *The Future Shape of Ministry,* by Urban T. Holmes.) Yet the real significance of this principle is not in the economics of church finance but is a theological assertion that Church office is essentially a matter of function within the body. To this assertion there is a corollary: no member of the body is without a function. We find this stated quite explicitly in one of the oldest Christian writings outside the New Testament:

The high priest is given his particular duties; the priests are assigned their special place, while on the Levites particular tasks are imposed. The layman is bound by the layman's code (1 Clement 40.5, trans. C.C. Richardson).

We would do well at this point to interject the distinction between spiritual gift and church office. Both exist and both are important, but the difference between them was not clearly marked in the early Church. Just as sacraments tended to be lumped together with sacred acts generally, the earliest Christians did not always distinguish between those who had been given a special endowment or *charisma* directly by God and those who had an official function in the body for which they had been set apart. Thus St. Paul said:

God has appointed in the church first apostles, second prophets, third teachers, then workers of miracles, then healers, helpers, administrators, and speakers in various kinds of tongues (1 Corinthians 12:28).

Some of these are obviously charismatics with powers of prophecy, miracle working, healing, and speaking with tongues. Since these gifts come from God, they come when he wants them to. That means that they can be very sporadic. For that reason the Church cannot depend on them for its day to day living. It must have regularly constituted channels through which it carries on its life and work as the community of salvation. These are what we call the Church officers. In St. Paul's list they include apostles, teachers, helpers, and administrators. In the Church as we know it today they are our ordained ministry of bishops, priests, and deacons. The power of God is manifested through these just as certainly as through the others; they are the regular channels of grace while the charismatic persons are special and occasional channels. With this background we can now move on to consider briefly the history of the Christian ministry.

The first point to remember in trying to understand the development of the Christian ministry is that Christianity grew out of Judaism. This is what Pope Pius XI meant in an address he made to Belgian pilgrims when he said, "Through Christ and in Christ, we are spiritual offspring of Abraham." It was probably not until at least thirty years after the Ascension, during the revolt of the Jews against Rome, that Christians began finally to separate themselves from Judaism. Indeed, recent research indicates that a very Jewish kind of Christianity played a much larger role in the early Church than was previously thought. Thus we must look for the roots of the Christian ministry in the Jewish.

The effort to do so, however, may be a little confusing since, from our point of view, the Jews had two kinds of ministry. One was the ministry of the Temple at Jerusalem. For at least six centuries before the time of Christ it had been lawful for Israelites to offer sacrifice in one place and in one place only and that was the Temple at Jerusalem. The sacrifices there were offered by the Temple priesthood. But not all Jewish worship was sacrificial; to make what must be a very inexact comparison, to the degree that their sacrifice corresponded to our eucharist, they had other services which corresponded to our daily offices of Morning and Evening Prayer. These services were those held in the synagogues that existed not only in Palestine but throughout the Mediterranean world of that day. It is from these services that we got not only our daily offices but also the service of the Word which begins the eucharist and, many scholars think, even the structure of the eucharistic prayer itself. These synagogue services were not conducted by priests; the synagogue was run by elders whose functions would probably seem to us more like those of vestrymen than those of clergy. But they did have the responsibility for seeing that the life of the synagogue, including its life of prayer and biblical study, was carried on. Thus we see that the Jewish religious community had two kinds of officers, what might be called in a very rough way the "sacramental" officers of the Temple at Jerusalem and the "non-sacramental," administrative officers in the synagogue. With this in mind, we must now digress briefly, but we will return to this point later.

The first people that we can call Christian ministers do not really belong to either type; they constitute a special category all their own. They are the twelve Apostles, who were appointed by our Lord for a unique ministry in relation to his own ministry. (We should point out here that some scholars question whether the term *apostle* was originally applied to the Twelve because it does not appear to have been applied to them by Paul, Mark, John, or Matthew.) The ministry of the Twelve seems to be divided into two periods: the lifetime of our Lord and the period after his resurrection and ascension. The first period is characterized in the story of their call as we read it in Mark 3:14–15: "And he appointed Twelve, to be with him, and to be sent out to preach, and have authority to cast out demons." The first thing that we need to notice here is the significance of the

number twelve. This was the number of the tribes of Israel.
The Gospels make it very clear to us that our Lord understood his role to be ushering in the kingdom or reign of God
on earth. His ministry is devoted to preaching the kingdom
of God to the Jews; he believed that when the Jews became
obedient, then the reign of God would burst into time and
would include all men. Thus the story of the call of the
Twelve suggests that Jesus intended for them to extend his
ministry while he was on earth; he sent them out to do what
he was doing—to preach the kingdom of God and to demonstrate its power in their mastery over demons and disease.
In the long run, their preaching was no better responded to
than his was; only a small part of Israel was obedient. Indeed, for a time, the part consisted of one man, Jesus himself,
but his obedience on the cross was enough to inaugurate the
reign of God which now exists in the world and which will
enter into its consummation at the end of the world. All of
that, however, is another story. The point we are interested
in now is that the Twelve had as their mission when Jesus
was on earth the extension of his ministry of proclaiming the
kingdom of God to Israel.

Their ministry after his departure is summarized in his
last words to them as quoted in Acts 1:8: "You shall receive
power when the Holy Spirit has come upon you; and you
shall be my witnesses in Jerusalem and in all Judea and
Samaria and to the end of the earth." As a result of having
been with him they could be witnesses to him, and thus expand the community of salvation which he had begun. While
we are to expect that the editorial hand of St. Luke is shown
not only in the phrasing of this sentence but in its concepts
as well, his reconstruction undoubtedly reflects something
of the historical role of the Twelve after the ascension. Since
the role of the Twelve was bearing witness to what they had
seen of Jesus' life, death, and resurrection, their ministry
died with them; there was no longer anyone qualified to give
an eyewitness report. Further, since the initial witness had

been made, there was no need to do it again; the charter witness of the Twelve would be what the Church would appeal to ever after as the basis of its faith. But while their particular ministry died with them, they did have the responsibility of founding the community in which other ministries would function.

In the Book of Acts we hear of how they began these other ministries. We read, for instance, that they appointed elders wherever they went. The use of the term *elder* reminds us of the organization of the Jewish synagogue and it should, because what the apostles did in effect was to set up Christian synagogues wherever they went, and these synagogues were governed by elders. As we saw above, the Greek word for elder is *presbyteros,* which is the root of the English word *presbyter* and, incidentally, the root also of *Presbyterian*— a person who believes that Church government should be by elders. This word *presbyter* was corrupted in its pronunciation through the centuries and our word *priest* is the result; one can see the progression from *presbyter* to *prester* (as in the legend of Prester John) to *priest.*

When we say priest we think first and foremost of authority to preside at the eucharistic celebration and that sounds very different from elder, but notice that our word priest is not derived either from the Greek *hiereus* nor from the Latin *sacerdos* (nor, for that matter, from the Hebrew *cohen*), the word in those languages used to designate the offerer of sacrifice. The reason that it is not derived from any of these is that the Christian presbyter was not the original offerer of the Christian sacrifice; that authority came to be delegated to him later, but originally it belonged to someone else. The first officer to whom the task is explicitly assigned in the records of the early Church that have come down to us is the bishop, though there were eucharists before there were bishops. It was the bishop, however, who delegated to presbyters the authority to preside at the Eucharist. We see the process of delegation in the letter of Ignatius of Antioch to

The famous "Chalice of Antioch," a silver, partially gilt chalice dating from the fourth or fifth century and found near Antioch. The relief carving on the chalice shows Christ preaching to his Apostles. It is one of the earliest known instances in Christian art where the Apostles are given individual identities. (Metropolitan Museum of Art, The Cloisters Collection, 1950.)

the church at Smyrna, written within twenty years after
the year 100 A.D.: "You should regard that eucharist as
valid which is celebrated either by the bishop or by someone
he authorizes" (8.1, trans. C. C. Richardson). We also see it
implied in the directions that Hippolytus gives for a new
bishop's first eucharist: "To him then the deacons shall bring
the offering, and he, laying his hand upon it with all the
presbytery, shall say as the thanksgiving . . ." (*Apostolic
Tradition* 4.2, trans. B. S. Easton).

The origin of deacons is a little more problematical than
that of elders, but there is good reason to believe that their
beginning is also related in the Book of Acts. Some difficulty
had arisen in the primitive Christian community at Jerusalem over the equitable distribution of food. The twelve
thought they had more pressing duties to perform than to
settle such squabbles.

The twelve summoned the body of the disciples and said, "It is
not right that we should give up preaching the word of God to
serve tables. Therefore, brethren, pick out from among you seven
men of good repute, whom we may appoint to this duty. But we
will devote ourselves to prayer and the ministry of the word"
(Acts 6:2–3).

While this story does not call the seven who were appointed
by the actual title of *deacons*, the task to which they were
appointed—that of administering alms—was characteristic
of deacons in the early Church and this passage has been
traditionally interpreted as referring to the institution of that
order. This interpretation is made more likely by the fact that
the Book of Acts does not afterwards mention any of the
seven functioning in the capacity for which they were appointed. The two who are noticed again, Stephen and Philip,
appear doing work more like that of the Apostles, the work
of the ministry of the word. Since the distribution of food
has no later importance in the Book of Acts, the only reason

we can imagine for the inclusion of the story is that it tells of how an important institution in the Church, the diaconate, was inaugurated. With the deacons, though, as with the elders, we see that an absolute distinction between a sacramental and a non-sacramental ministry does not hold up. The quotation we have just read from Hippolytus shows that both deacons and elders had their distinctive ministry to perform in the celebration of the Eucharist.

Bishops are mentioned in the New Testament, but it is difficult to tell precisely what their relation to the other clergy was. Perhaps McKenzie is right in regarding the overseers (as the Greek word *episkopoi* means) as "an executive board of the elders" (*Authority in the Church*, p. 72). Certainly the word occurs in the plural in Acts and Philippians as it does also in 1 Clement, so that we are left with the impression that in the earliest days there was more than one bishop in the church in each city. It appears that in the earliest days the chief authorities in the Church were not tied down to one place but were itinerant. An Apostle such as St. Paul had charge of a large mission field. We hear too, especially in the *Didache,* of prophets and teachers who were itinerant, but who could settle down in one place. When there was no itinerant officer of universal authority present, such as an Apostle, prophet, or teacher, responsibility in the local church was exercised perhaps by the elders or by an executive board such as McKenzie suggests who came to be called *overseers.* In time the authority of the group would tend to fall more and more upon one member and he would become the overseer *par excellence,* what scholars refer to as a "monarchical bishop."

There have been a number of writers who have seen a resemblance between the bishop of the early Church and an official of the community that produced the Dead Sea Scrolls who was called the *mebaqqer,* a rare word in Hebrew which means something similar to what *episkopos* means in Greek. Two main differences between the two offices have been pointed out by A. R. C. Leaney: the first is that the *mebaqqer* appears to have no pastoral duties as the bishop certainly did and the second is that the *mebaqqer* "seems to be an indispensable camp overseer acting as a kind of public prosecutor for the whole community in cases of transgressions of the Law" while "we cannot imagine that the (bishop) counted among his chief duties the presentation of a case against an offender" (*The Rule of Qumran and Its Meaning*, p. 189). Yet we have seen that the correspondence between Christian clergy and their Jewish antecedents is not exact and it remains possible that the office of *mebaqqer* did have some influence on the origin of the episcopate.

One question to which the answer is far from clear is, as we have already indicated, who presided at the eucharist during the New Testament period. It is impossible to imagine, in the light of Jewish order in such matters, that the opportunity was open to every member of the community. There is much to be said for the suggestion of C. F. D. Moule:

It is natural to assume that an apostle would preside (or at least be invited to preside), if present. The prestige of the Twelve, as eyewitnesses commissioned by the Lord to give evidence of the Gospel facts, may be assumed to have set them at the head of a congregation assembled for worship (*Worship in the New Testament*, p. 29).

When there was no apostle present (which would have been most of the time, for the apostles were itinerant church officers), it is very likely that the president was one of the elders or bishops, though not necessarily always the same one. A bishop's collegial sharing of his presidential liturgy may have survived vestigially in the days shortly after the disappearance of the apostles, when one bishop was at the head of each local church. In the notation by Ignatius, quoted above, the bishop was permitted to delegate his presidency to another, while in the direction given by Hippolytus, the elders should join the bishop in laying hands on the "offering." Certainly the oldest documents which do identify the celebrant designate him as the bishop.

The first clear pictures of the ministry we get comes to us from around the year 200 A.D., which, of course, gives us a stable ministry before we got our creeds or even our list of the books that constitute the New Testament. The picture we get is something like this. For some time there was a bishop over the church in every city. He presided over the worship of the community but he had a council of elders to help him with the government of the church. The deacons assisted him in the conduct of worship and in the administration of charity and hospitality. This, as we said, is the earliest clear picture we have of the Church's ministry. This takes us up to the point where all of the major orders of ministry are in existence. Thus we have completed what Dom Gregory Dix called the "constitutional" history of the ministry ("The Ministry in the Early Church," *The Apostolic Ministry*, ed. K. E. Kirk, p. 189). In the next chapter we will go on to consider the "administrative" history of the ministry, the story of the evolution of the organization of the Church.

A silver repoussé plaque depicting the Apostle Paul carrying a book. Found near Antioch, it dates from the sixth century. (Metropolitan Museum of Art, Fletcher Fund, 1950.)

9

The Genesis of the Church

The question of how we got our Church has
an answer that in a sense is obvious: God gave
it to us. This is the ultimate theological answer
to all of the questions of Christian origins in the entire book.
Yet God seldom intervenes directly into human affairs; his
mighty acts in history are normally accomplished through
human mediation. It is of such historical causation that we
will speak in the present chapter too, although the assumption of God's primary agency will now be a little more obviously the context of all that we say.

In order to be able to answer the question of how we
got our Church we must ask the preliminary question of
when the Church got started. This second question was
phrased in a slightly different way by a great Church historian of the last century, Dean A. P. Stanley. He asked:
"Where does Ecclesiastical History commence?" And the
answer he gives is a revealing one. He points out that we
could, with some show of reason, begin at the Reformation
or the Middle Ages or with the early Church Fathers. But,
he tells us, we need really to go back to the time of Abraham;
the beginning of Christianity goes back to the beginning of
Israel (*Lectures on the History of the Eastern Church*, p. 6).

Perhaps we can get some insight into why this is so by
looking at the derivation of a word. Dean Stanley called
church history *ecclesiastical history*. It means the same thing,

of course; ecclesiastical is an adjective meaning "of or per-
taining to the Church." It is derived from the Greek word
ekklesia which we translate *church*. But this word *ekklesia*
itself has a derivation; it is a compound word, the components of which are a verb that means *to call* and a preposi-
tion that means *out*. Thus the Church is that community
which is "called out." We may trace our word origin a bit
further. This word *ekklesia* is used in the Greek version of
the Old Testament to translate a Hebrew word that is used
to designate the people of God. The Hebrew word is *qahal*
and it too is related to a verb meaning *to call*. The Church,
then, is that community which is called into existence by
God.

We have spoken before of the Church as the community
of salvation in which we enter into interpersonal encounter
and fellowship with God. God created man so that he could
enjoy the supreme benefit of that fellowship. God did this
because "it belongs to the very nature of the good to extend
itself, to stretch itself, to give itself away." The Bible teaches
us in the story of the Garden of Eden that man turned his
back on God and refused his proffer of friendship, but the
determination of God to share himself was not to be frus-
trated. Time and again he called to man, called him back to
the paradisal community that he had forsaken. The story of
Noah, for instance, is the story of such an effort to begin
again.

It is with Abraham, however, that we have the real beginning of the historical community of which we are members.

By faith Abraham obeyed when he was called to go out to a
place which he was to receive as an inheritance; and he went out,
not knowing where he was to go. By faith he sojourned in the
land of promise, as in a foreign land, living in tents with Isaac and
Jacob, heirs with him of the same promise. For he looked forward to a city which has foundations, whose builder and maker
is God (Hebrews 11:8–10).

Then Moses was called to begin again, to lead God's people out of the land of bondage and to bring them into the land promised by God, the land flowing with milk and honey. Even here in the promised land, though, they were not all faithful; many "went a whoring after other gods" (Judges 2:17, King James version). In so doing they went again into captivity. The prophets had warned them that it would be so, but with this oracle of doom they also prophesied that God would not forsake his people forever.

Therefore, behold, the days are coming, says the Lord, when men shall no longer say, 'As the Lord lives who brought up the people of Israel out of the land of Egypt,' but 'As the Lord lives who brought up and led the descendants of the house of Israel out of the north country and out of all the countries where he had driven them.' Then they shall dwell in their own land (Jeremiah 23:7–8).

Out of the nation that God had called into being and then called to be his own, only a remnant remained. And, as time went on, even that remnant dwindled. The community of salvation that God had called out had to be begun all over again. It was not to be the "new" Israel—the New Testament never calls it that—but the true Israel, the community that God had been calling out from the very beginning. This new period of the history of the community of salvation is the period in which the community is called the Christian Church.

The Epistle to the Hebrews begins its discussion of the relation of the new covenant God made with his people in Jesus Christ to the old covenant of the Old Testament with these words:

In many and various ways God spoke of old to our fathers by the prophets; but in these last days he has spoken to us by a Son whom he has appointed the heir of all things, through whom also he created the world (1:1–2).

One of the New Testament ways of speaking of this relation between God and his *qahal,* his *ekklesia,* is in terms of the remnant spoken of by the prophets. The remnant of the faithful is seen to have dwindled progressively until it consisted exclusively of one man and that man was on the cross. The earliest gospel to be written down, that of St. Mark, may be read as a record of the estrangement of Jesus, first from the religious leaders of his people, then from his own family, and next from some of his followers, so that finally he was bereft of even his closest disciples. But as the faithful remnant of Israel—even though that remnant consisted of only one person—he was Israel; all Israel was present in his person. What he did on the cross he did as a representative person who had power of attorney for the whole community. At that moment the community consisted of him alone but all of those who were later to be initiated into the community would benefit from what he did there. On the cross Jesus was the community called by God. In Hebrew the same verb means both to hear and to obey; in Jesus the community called by God heard his call and was obedient to it. Thus there was accomplished the full restoration of the fellowship that had been broken in Eden. As St. Paul said, "For as by one man's disobedience many were made sinners, so by one man's obedience many will be made righteous" (Romans 5:19). Or again, "For as in Adam all die, so also in Christ shall all be made alive" (1 Corinthians 15:22).

Because during the lifetime of Jesus the Church consisted of him alone, the word *Church* occurs only a few times in the Gospels. There it refers to the future Christian community. This community came into existence on the day of Pentecost when the Holy Spirit came down upon the disciples and filled them with his power. Being filled with the Holy Spirit had characterized Jesus during his lifetime and it became characteristic of the Church after his Ascension. It could be said that it was his possession of the Spirit that constituted him as the Church and that it was by passing the Spirit on to his followers that he included them in this restored Israel. The Church, then, is the Spirit-filled community. And, as we said when we were discussing sacraments of initiation, the story of the Book of Acts is the story of the extension of the Spirit-filled community throughout the known world—in Jerusalem, in all Judea and Samaria, and to the end of the earth.

Thus in the Book of Acts the word *church* has two distinguishable but closely connected meanings. It can refer to the whole Church, the Spirit-filled community gradually extended throughout the Roman Empire, and it can refer also to the local congregations of Christians founded by the apostles. K. L. Schmidt has stated in an admirable way the relation of the local groups to the universal community:

It is not that the *ekklesia* is divided into *ekklesiai* (plural). It is not that the *ekklesiai* are added up to make the *ekklesia*. Rather, the *ekklesia* is to be found in the places named (Article on *ekklesia* in *Theological Dictionary of the New Testament*, ed. G. Kittel, trans. G. W. Bromiley, III, 505).

Each congregation is a local embodiment of the universal Church.

That reminds us of our definition of the Church as the community of salvation in which there occurs personal encounter with God. Dom Gregory Dix said it this way: "Until the third century the word 'church' means invariably . . . the solemn assembly for the liturgy, and by extension those who have a right to take a part in this" (*Shape of the Liturgy*, p. 19). Thus the liturgical assembly is the local embodiment of the whole people of God. This is the community, called by God to have fellowship with him, actually engaged in that fellowship.

This means, of course, that we cannot think of worship as one activity among many others in which the Church engages. It is specifically in its worship that the Church is the

Church, is the community called by God into fellowship with himself. Thus there is a way in which it is true to say that the Church comes into existence when her people assemble for worship, that their coming together creates the body anew. This does not mean that worship was the only thing that Christians did together. Rather the pagan world was amazed at how the Christians loved one another. This shock is described by Adolf Harnack:

Such a religious and social organization, destitute of any political or national basis and yet embracing the entire private life, was a novel and unheard-of thing upon the soil of Greek and Roman life, where religious and social organizations only existed as a rule in a quite rudimentary form, and where they lacked any religious control of life as a whole. . . . But here was a society which united fellow-believers, who were resident in any city, in the closest of ties, presupposing a relationship which was assumed as a matter of course to last through life itself, furnishing its members . . . with a daily bond which provided them with spiritual benefits and imposed duties on them, assembling them daily at first and then weekly, shutting them off from other people, uniting them in a guild of worship, a friendly society, and an order with a definite line of life in view, besides teaching them to consider themselves as the community of God (*Mission and Expansion of Christianity*, pp. 432f.).

It was this sense of being the community of God that made all of the other unity possible and desirable.

The importance of worship in the early Church is what makes the ministry so important. As we said in the last chapter, the New Testament does not identify the officers who presided over the eucharists of the primitive Church, but when they are identified, they are called bishops. Thus the bishop was the center of unity in the local church. This is made abundantly clear in the letters of St. Ignatius of Antioch, a Syrian bishop who wrote when he was on the way to martyrdom in Rome half a century after the martyrdom of

St. Peter and St. Paul there. He makes such statements as these:

Nobody must do anything that has to do with the Church without the bishop's approval. You should regard that eucharist as valid which is celebrated either by the bishop or by someone he authorizes. Where the bishop is present, there let the congregation gather, just as where Jesus Christ is, there is the Catholic Church (*Smyrnaeans* 8, trans. C. C. Richardson).

The importance of the bishop is seen to extend so far that he is to be consulted by young people about whom they should marry and by slaves seeking their freedom. The bishop is advised by his council of elders and assisted in his liturgical and charitable duties by the deacons. This division of labor and responsibility could even be seen in the arrangement of furniture in the earliest churches. The altar in these churches was a portable table brought in for the purpose. Behind the table was a semicircular row of seats—say maybe seven of them—in which the elders sat. The center seat, directly facing the people, was the bishop's chair. The deacons, being helpers, stood.

The conversion of Constantine and the christianization of the Roman empire did cause some very basic changes in the organization of the Church, though. Many readers were undoubtedly surprised to note that the chief minister of the local congregation was a bishop; they probably thought that the regular president at the eucharist sounded more like a parish priest than a bishop. At this time, though, while the Christians were not in such constant danger of persecution as we may have thought, they still dared not be as open as to have any elaborate overall organization. The universal Church was a number of local units that had only a certain amount of communication with one another. The head of the congregation in a particular city was the bishop. After Christianity became legal—and even state-supported—all this changed. The Church began to expand at a rapid rate. The parishes in the large cities would start missions in the suburbs and then in the small towns nearby. There began to be Christians who lived too far from the church in the city to attend the eucharist there. The only alternative was to send the eucharist to them. The bishop would delegate his elders to become the regular officiants at the eucharist in the smaller congregations. At first he was still the chief pastor of the city and its environs. For a while the bishop of Rome would consecrate enough breads at mass to send one to each of the other Roman churches as a sign of unity. But the direction of the evolution is clear; eventually the bishop became the spiritual father of not one congregation but of a number. Thus he became the head of what we would call a diocese instead of a parish. Then, as time went on, the bishops in the vicinity of a large city would recognize their subordination to the bishop of that city—the metropolitan or patriarch or archbishop as he would be called. Thus developed the organization of the Church as we know it today except for the changes wrought by our unhappy divisions which make it possible for there to be several bishops in a single city, each the head of a different community of Christians.

The fact that we have brought Church history up to our own time, however, does not mean that Church history is over. The community of salvation will last until the consummation of the present age. Even then, though, the Church will not be over even if history is. The Church will abide throughout ages of ages. The Church as we know it on earth is the Church still fighting, the Church in transit, the pilgrim Church. But the destination of the Church has always been the destination of Abraham, "the city which has foundations, whose builder and maker is God" (Hebrews 11:10). The Revelation of St. John the Divine is a vision of the heavenly city and it is a city in which the community of salvation truly has encounter with the God that called it out. And this encounter is described by St. John in terms of worship:

Then I heard what seemed to be the voice of a great multitude, like the sound of many waters, and like the sound of mighty thunderpeals, crying,

> Hallelujah! For the Lord Our God Almighty reigns.
> Let us rejoice and exult and give him glory,
> For the marriage of the Lamb has come,
> And his bride has made herself ready;

It was granted her to be clothed with fine linen, bright and pure —for the fine linen is the righteous deeds of the saints (19:6–8).

This then is the divine-human encounter that awaits the community of salvation at the consummation of the age, the marriage of the Lamb of God to his bride, the Church.

Epilogue

As I think of the consummation of the Church in its beauty at the end of the present age, I cannot help but think of it as it is presently in its pilgrim state, torn asunder by many divisions. It must have been obvious all the way through that this book was written from the perspective of the Episcopal Church; illustrations have been drawn from its life, its structure has determined the format, and my findings have been stated in the language of its vocabulary. I, and all its members, rejoice that the Episcopal Church participates in the great tradition that I have described. Yet the discerning eye must have observed something else; it must have been clear that none of the institutions described exists in precisely the same form in any modern communion as that which it had in the period discussed. What I have written has been in the spirit of Fr. Bonnell Spencer, O.H.C., who said:

The day should soon be passed when any portion of the divided Church, no matter how large it is or how certain it may have been that it alone has faithfully preserved primitive precedents, will hope to achieve reunion on the basis of its own position, with no more than a sympathetic understanding and forgiveness of its erring brethren, coupled perhaps with some allowance for and adaptation of their principal affirmations (*Sacrifice of Thanksgiving*, pp. 6f.).

I have spoken of the consummation of the Church at the end of the age. There is another, lesser, and yet immensely important, consummation to which the Church must also look forward, and that, pray God, at a time before the end. That consummation is the restoration of visible unity to the Church, the mending of the many tears in the seamless robe of Christ.

Bibliography

GENERAL REFERENCE WORKS ON THE BIBLE:

Theological Dictionary of the New Testament. Ed. Gerhard Kittel and Gerhard Friedrich, trans. G.W. Bromiley. Grand Rapids: Eerdmans. A massive monument of German biblical scholarship that gives an exhaustive treatment of the theologically significant words in the Greek New Testament. Very technical.

Hans Conzelmann. *Outline of the Theology of the New Testament.* Trans. John Bowden. New York: Harper & Row, 1969. Exactly what the title says except that it is in essay form rather than a bare list of topics. Done by one of the best New Testament scholars of today.

CHRISTIAN THEOLOGY:

E. Schillebeeckx. *Christ the Sacrament of Encounter with God.* New York: Sheed & Ward, 1963. The work that has most influenced the thought of this book.

C.S. Lewis. *Mere Christianity.* New York: Macmillan, 1952. One of the most lucid and charming defenses of Christian belief ever to appear.

R.A. Norris. *God and World in Early Christian Theology.* New York: Seabury Press, 1965. A lucid exposition of the thought of the first Christian theologians as they entered into a dialogue with contemporary pagan thought.

EARLY CHRISTIAN HISTORY:

A New Eusebius. Ed. J. Stevenson. London: SPCK-Seabury, 1957. A very useful collection of the main documents used in reconstructing the early history and doctrine of the Church.

Adolf von Harnack. *The Mission and Expansion of Christianity in the First Three Centuries.* Trans. and ed. by James Moffatt. New York: Harper & Row, 1961 (reprint of the first volume of the London edition of 1908). A "practical" history of the early Church concentrating on the factors that made it possible for Christianity to spread so rapidly.

Early Christian Fathers. Ed. C.C. Richardson. "Library of Christian Classics." Philadelphia: Westminster Press, 1953. Some of the major Christian writings from the century after the New Testmament period—in translation, with notes.

Hippolytus. *The Apostolic Tradition.* Trans. with notes by B.S. Easton. Cambridge: Cambridge University Press, 1934. Report of the liturgy of the church in Rome at the end of the second century.

133

HISTORY OF RELIGIONS:

Mircea Eliade, *Sacred and Profane*. New York: Harper & Row, 1961. A study of the division of all things into two spheres by religious man.

_____. *Cosmos and History*. New York: Harper & Row, 1959. A documentation of the thesis that the religion of primitive man is designed to take him back to the time of creation to restore his original power.

_____. *Birth and Rebirth*. New York: Harper & Row, 1958. An analysis of the "rites of passage" and initiation.

THEORY OF HISTORY:

R.G. Collingwood. *The Idea of History*. New York: Oxford University Press, 1946. The work which revolutionized thought about the nature of history.

THE BIBLE:

Robert M. Grant. *The Formation of the New Testament*. New York: Harper & Row, 1965. A popular history of the process of canonizing the New Testament written by a foremost New Testament scholar.

CREEDS:

J.N.D. Kelly. *Early Christian Creeds*. London: Longmans, Green & Co., 1950. The classic study on which our treatment is based.

_____. *The Athanasian Creed*. New York: Harper & Row, 1964. The same scholar's study of the *Quicunque vult*.

Massey Shepherd, *The Worship of the Church*. New York: Seabury.

CHURCH ARCHITECTURE:

Richard Krautheimer. *Early Christian and Byzantine Architecture*. "Pelican History of Art." Baltimore: Penguin Books, 1965. Massive, beautiful, and learned.

William MacDonald. *Early Christian and Byzantine Architecture*. "The Great Ages of World Architecture." New York: George Braziller, 1965. A much shorter but still very good treatment of the same subject.

Basil Minchin. *Outward and Visible*. London: Darton:, Longman, & Todd, 1961. A history of Church building told from the liturgical rather than the architectural point of view.

LITURGY:

Louis Bouyer. *Liturgical Piety*. Notre Dame: University of Notre Dame Press, 1955. The volume that had most to do with spreading the modern liturgical movement.

C.F.D. Moule. *Worship in the New Testament*. "Ecumenical Studies in Worship." Richmond: John Knox Press, 1961. A great New Testament scholar from Cambridge follows out the clues that the Bible gives about how the first Christians worshipped.

J.A. Jungmann. *Early Liturgy, to the Time of Gregory the Great*. Notre Dame: University of Notre Dame Press, 1959. A clasic study.

Theodor Klauser. *A Short History of the Western Liturgy*. New York: Oxford Press, 1969. A short handbook by a great scholar.

Gregory Dix. *Shape of the Liturgy*. London: Dacre, 1945. The great ground-breaking work by the noted Anglican Benedictine scholar.

_____. *Worship of the Church*. "The Church's Teaching." New York: Seabury Press. 1952. A presentation for lay people of the liturgy of the Prayer Book.

CHRISTIAN INITIATION:

Charles Davis. *Sacraments of Initiation: Baptism and Confirmation*. New York: Sheed & Ward, 1964. A theological and historical study by an English Roman Catholic theologian who has since been secularized.

Burkhard Neunheuser. *Baptism and Confirmation*. Trans. John Jay Hughes. "Herder History of Dogma." New York: Herder & Herder, 1964. A thorough historical survey.

THE EUCHARIST:

Helmer Ringgren. *Sacrifice in the Bible*. London: Lutterworth Press, 1963. A convenient summary of the background in Jewish sacrifice that Christians now recognize the Eucharist to have.

Joachim Jeremias. *Eucharistic Words of Jesus*. Trans. Norman Perrin. New York: Charles Scribner's Sons, 1966. Although individual scholars might question details, this is still the definitive treatment of Jesus' institution of the Eucharist.

Bonnell Spencer. *Sacrifice of Thanksgiving*. West Park, N.Y.: Holy Cross, 1965. A clear and sympathetic statement of contemporary thought about the sacrament by an Episcopal monk and liturgical scholar.

MINOR SACRAMENTS:

B. Poschmann. *Penance and the Anointing of the Sick*. "Herder History of Dogma." New York: Herder & Herder, 1964. Thorough historical study.

MINISTRY:

Urban T. Holmes. *The Future Shape of Ministry*. New York: Seabury Press, 1971. Masterful blending of historical, theological, and social science data to project the direction that the ordained ministry will take in the future.

John L. McKenzie. *Authority in the Church*. New York: Sheed and Ward. 1966. The best thing I know on the scriptural attitude toward ministry.

A.R.C. Leaney. *The Rule of Qumran and Its Meaning*. London: SCM, 1965. The place to get set straight about possible influences of the dead Sea Scrolls sect on the ministry of the early Church.